Handbook for Competitive Examinations in Library And Information Science

HANDBOOK FOR COMPETITIVE EXAMINATIONS IN LIBRARY AND INFORMATION SCIENCE

Edited and Compiled by
Prof. A.A.N.Raju

Ess Ess Publications
New Delhi

Handbook for Competitive Examinations in Library And Information Science

Copyright © by Editor

All rights reserved. No part of this book may be reproduced in any form or by any electronic or mechanical means including information storage and retrieval systems without permission in writing from the publisher, except by a reviewer, who may quote brief passages in a review.

While extensive effort has gone into ensuring the reliability of information appearing in this book, the publisher makes no warranty, express or implied on the accuracy or reliability of the information, and does not assume and hereby disclaims any liability to any person for any loss or damage caused by errors or omissions in this publication.

ISBN : 978-81-947398-4-5

First Published 2021

Price : Rs. 950/-

Published by:
Ess Ess Publications
4831/24, Ansari Road,
Darya Ganj,
New Delhi-110 002.
INDIA
Phones: 23260807, 41563444
Fax: 41563334
E-mail: info@essessreference.com
www.essessreference.com

Cover Design by *Patch Creative Unit*

Printed and bound in India

Contents

Preface

Acknowledgements

Concepts (A - Z)   1 - 280

Preface

The subject Library and Information Science (LIS) is being taught at Post-Graduate level in about hundred Universities including Open and Distance Learning Universities / Institutes offering MLISc, M.Phil and Ph.D. degrees. To recruit trained manpower at different levels and award of Fellowships and other types of scholarships many National and State level Institutions, Government Departments and other agencies have been conducting recruitment / eligibility tests. In this regard mention may be made of University Grant Commission's (UGC's) Eligibility Test (NET) for according eligibility for the appointment of Assistant Professors in all subject fields including LIS and Assistant Librarians (now Assistant Professors) for University and College Libraries.

The NET is also the basis for the award of Junior Research Fellowships (JRF) to pursue research degrees leading to the award of M.Phil and Ph.D. degrees by the Universities and institutions of higher learning in the Country. The NET is compulsory for those who wish to apply for the post of Lecturer / Assistant Librarian in the Universities of our Country. Many of the States in the Country have adopted the NET model and conducting similar eligibility tests for the recruitment of Lecturers / Librarians in Government Degree Colleges. Some of the State Public Service Commissions and College Service Commissions have also been conducting eligibility tests slightly modifying the NET pattern and syllabus to meet their local needs and requirements.

The topics / concepts listed have been selected from articles appeared in the leaned Library and Information Journals such as *SRELS Journal of Information Management, IFLA Journal, International Journal of Information Dissemination and Technology, Indian Journal of Information, Library and Society, Annals of Library and Information Studies,* and *DESIDOC Journal of Library & Information Technology*. Emphasis has been given to Information Technology. The Compilation includes about 860 topics / concepts.

For objective questions in LIS one may refer to **Objective Question Bank for Library and Information Science Ability Tests**, 2nd Revised and Enlarged Edition, 2005 by Prof. A. A. N. Raju and Published by Ess Ess Publications, New Delhi, 2005.

The Editor / Compiler believes that these concepts (topics) will be of great help to those candidates appearing for various competitive tests in Library and Information Science. It acts as a ready reckoner as the topics / concepts are arranged alphabetically.

Hyderabad **PROF. A.A.N.RAJU**

Acknowledgements

At the outset I would like to thank Dr. A. R. Chakravarthy, Asst. Professor, Osmania University Library, who provided me back volumes of LIS Journals listed in the preface. I would also like to thank Sri M. Madhusudan (Madhu) who helped in the preparation of press copy. Lastly but not the least I thank the dynamic Managing Director of M/s Ess Ess Publications, Sri Sumit Sethi, who came forward to undertake this publication in spite of difficult publication scenario in the Country.

— ***Editor***

A

ACG-LMS

This is a library maintenance software named Library Management System developed and marketed by ACG InfoTech Ltd. It is built upon client-server architecture and provides GUI interface that requires little or no patron training. ACG-LMS's access restrictions allows each staff member to be restricted at database record and even field level Management functions can also be limited for each user. Users are not able to alter data from OPAC model. LMS controls access to all functions of the system and gives each staff member a unique set of operational rights. Its Operating Environment Server is Windows NTG. Client Workstations: Windows 95 / 98, Remote clients: RAS. The software supports various platforms such as MSSQL 7.0, Visual Basic 6.0 and Crystal Reports. The Company also undertakes retro-conversion job in addition to the installation of software at a cost of Rs.300,000 to Rs.3,50,000 for a college library having a collection of 100,000 books / bound volumes of periodicals.

AGRICOLA

AGRICOLA (Agricultural on-line Access) is a machine readable base of bibliographic citations created by National Agricultural Library (NAL), Belts Ville, USA and its co-operators. The scope of this database encompasses all aspects of agriculture and allied disciplines and abstracts are prepared from material received either at NAL or its co-operations. The database includes about 90% of the records from journal articles and book chapters and the remaining 10% describe monographs, series, microforms, audio-visuals, maps and other types of material.

AGRIS

Agricultural Research Information System (AGRIS) is an

international bibliographic information system for the agricultural sciences and technology. It was created in 1974 by the FAO of the United Nations to facilitate information exchange and provide bibliographical control of the world literature dealing with all aspects of agriculture. The AGRIS database is an enormous collection of 2.6 million structured bibliographical records. The system is centrally managed by the WAICENT / FAOINFO Dissemination Management Branch of the Library and Documentation Systems, Division (GIL) of FAO of UN. It is a cooperative system in which participation countries input the references to the literature / documents produced within their boundaries and in turn, get an access to the information provided by the other participants. The database contains 75% journal articles, 18% monographs, 6% Conference Papers and 1% other literature. About 159 national, 31 International and inter-governmental centers participate and submit about 14,000 items per month. The bibliographic inputs received from participating countries are collected and processed in the AGRIS processing Unit, Vienna which is hosted by the Division of Scientific and Technical Information of the International Atomic Energy Agency (IAEA).

ADINET (Ahmedabad Library Network)

It was formally inaugurated in February 1995 when a memorandum of understanding (MOU) was signed between NISSAT and ADINET at Ahmedabad. It is the 5th library network sponsored by NISSAT in the Country and aims to bring about cooperative mode of working among more than 150 libraries and information centres in and around Ahmedabad. Adopting modern tools of information technology ADINET will not only help library users but individuals too, of different professions in getting access to information of their choice and interest. Coordinated efforts for suitable collection development will result in appreciable reduction of unnecessary duplication of periodical subscriptions. E-mail facility being provided by ADINET will enable the member to exchange information with others within the city and outside. *Services:* 1. Library related services: Online information search, inter-library loan, photocopying service, current awareness service and information services. 2. Other services: E-mail serving and Bulletin Board Service.

AICTE (The All India Council for Technical Education)

The All India Council for Technical Education has been in existence since November 1945 as a national level APEX Advisory Body with its mission of developing and promoting quality technical education in the Country. The AICTE Act 1987 was passed by Parliament of India for the establishment of AICTE with a view to ensure proper planning and coordinated development of Technical Education in the Country.

Abstract

"Description in a summary form, of the subject content of a documents (e.g. Journal article) without added interpretation or criticism, produced in order to facilitate users access to the information (through the condensation of the primary document) and its storage and retrieval". *(UNISIST Document).*

Abstracting Service

It is a service which covers a defined subject area and examines the primary literature of that subject area for the purpose of summarizing that literature by means of abstract entries. E.g. Sociological Abstract, Geo-Abstracts, Economics Abstracts, Library and Information Science Abstracts (LISA).

Academic Status of librarians

It may be as the formal recognition in writing by an institution's authorities of librarians as members of the instructional and research staff. The recognition may take the form of assigned faculty ranks and titles or equivalent ranks and titles according to institutional custom.

Accountability

1. "It is an action of a person or organization to be taken or made towards the achievement of goals and responsibility is what must be done by a person. In nutshell accountability is answerable for an action, where responsibility is what one must do". (P. Proctor).
2. "Accountability is to be considered as obligation to give an account of one's performance in the form of report or some other form of explanation or exposition. It is a meant to answer for one's action taken by him to achieve the objectives". (R. B. Wagner).

Accreditation

1. It is a Voluntary System of evaluation of higher educational Institutions and programmes. It is a collegial process based on self-evaluation and peer assessment for improvement of academic quality and public accountability. It assures that higher educational institutions and their units, scholars or programs meet appropriate standards of quality and integrity.
2. It refers to "approval or recognition of one party by another on the basis of some standards" (Kent and Lancour).

Adult education

"The effort put forthby mature person to improve himself by acquiring new skills, information understanding, attitude or appreciations of the efforts of an agency to present the opportunity and the encouragement to mature persons for improving themselves or their community (Houle)

Advice Blog

It is weblog that provides expert advice such as personal

finance blog (Mint life) or parenting and family blog (The Mother Load).

Aggregator

An aggregator is a database, collection of electronic publications, most commonly a searchable collection of electronic journals. It provides access to a large number of e-journals range of different publications.

Characteristics : 1. Convenient, 2. Accessibility, 3. Coverage, 4. Credibility.

Alice for Windows

This software was developed by SoftLink Asia, Pvt. Ltd. This software had tried to match international standards. A multi user package costed Rs.1,50,000/- for 5 Nodes. For each additional node, the Company charged Rs.10,000/-. The software can be run on LAN using Windows NT Server or Novell Netware and for nodes Windows NT Workstation or Windows 95 / 98. It also provides Manual to run the software. It was an Australian product.

Altmetrics

It is also known as Alternative Matrics (ALM) or Alt-matrics. A relatively new term that was coined in 2010 by Jason Priem as an alternative way of measuring impact in the social web and aims at enhancing and complementing the more traditional way of impact assessment by expanding the idea of impact.

It is a growing measure for academic impact and it is gaining worldwide importance. The aim is to measure impact of scholars and scholarly documents not captured by traditional bibliometrics which are usually restricted to counting peer reviewed journal articles and citations within them.

Altmetric.com

It analyses the online impact of research articles based on a variety of sources, generates a score and conveys this information through small donut shaped visualizations for fast comprehension. It collects data about an individual article and supplied this data to publishers.

Altmetrics.org

This free Website is a Central hub for information about the growing altmetrics movement. It maintains links to new online tools for calculating impact. Its other prominent features include an altmetrics 'manifesto' that argue to show that altmetrics can improve existing scholarly filters.

Amazon Web Services (AWS)

This is perceived as one of major players in the business offering a wide range of prominent cloud computing services such as elastic compute cloud (EC2), simple storage service (S3) simple DB and simple queuing service (SQS). It provides a reliable, scalable, low-cost infrastructure platform in the cloud that powers hundreds of thousands businesses in Countries around the World.

Android

It is a Linux-based operating system primarily designed for mobile devices such a smart phones and tablet computers utilizing ARM Processors. A secondary target for the light weight O.S. is embedded systems such as networking equipment, smart T.V. Systems including set top boxes. It has become the World's leading smart phone platform at the end of 2010. Android 4.1, Jally Bean is the fastest and smoothest version of Android yet.

Application Software

It is the most critical subsystem in Library Automation and the success of automation depends on its correct implementation. Library Management Software, developed commercially and institutionally deals with various housekeeping activities of the library: Creation of databases and information retrieval and dissemination. Some of the software packages available in India were: 1. CDS / ISIS, 2. LIBRIS, 3. Maitraiya, 4. TULIPS, 5. LIBSYSIS, 6. DELMS.

Archives

1. Archives are all those records irrespective of their physical form which are generally preserved on account of their enduring value by an organization or an individual responsible for its creation.
2. "A body of non-current permanently valuable records, applied also to their place of deposit or a building dedicated to their care and use, and to the organization or agency responsible for administering them" (J. B. Roads).

Physical Forms : 1. Manuscripts, 2. Cartographic and architectural records, 3. A.V. Materials, 4. Machine-readable records, and 5. Printed archives.

Characteristics : 1. Archives bear a special relationship to their creating agency, 2. Archives bear official character, 3. Archives have their uniqueness. No record copy or copies of these are available, 4. Organic character.

Categories : 1. According to character, 2. According to form, 3. According to legitimate use, 4. According to state of compilation, 5. According to subject matter, 6. Accord to importance, 7. According to chronological limits.

Artificial Intelligence (AI)

1. It is the study of mental facilities through the use of computational models.
2. "AI is a branch of computer science concerned with the study and creation of computer systems that exhibit some form of intelligence: Systems which learn new

concepts and tasks, systems that can reason and draw useful conclusions about the world around us, systems that can understand a natural language or perceive and comprehend a visual scene and systems that perform other types of feats that require human types of intelligence" (D. W.Patterson).

3. "The science and engineering of making intelligent machines, especially intelligent computer programmes" (John McCarthy).

Main goals : 1. To create expert systems – the systems which exhibit intelligent behavior, learn, demonstrate, explain and advice its users and 2. To implement human intelligence in machines – to create systems that understand, think, learn and behave like humans. (Gupta and Dhawan).

Artificial Neural Network (ANN)

It is an information processing paradigm that is inspired by the way biological nervous system, such as, the brain, process information. The key element of this paradigm is the novel structure of the information processing system. It is composed of a large number of highly interconnected processing elements (neurons) working in unison to solve specific problems.

Assistive Technologies

Refer to products, devices and equipment that are used to maintain, increase or improve functional capabilities of people with disabilities (Koulikourdi).

Attribute

"An attribute is a characteristic, a property or a fact of an entity, entity class or entity-type and a set of attributes described an entity or entity type" (S. R. Ranganathan).

Audio blog

It is MP3 blog which makes audio files valuable to the

user. It is normally targeted at highly specialized musical genres such as late 60's soul music or early 90's hip-hop.

Author

1. "Person creating the work, that is thought and expression constituting it". (S. R. Ranganathan).
2. "The Person chiefly responsible for the creation of the intellectual or artistic content of a work" (AACR-II).
3. "Creator of a work, the person or corporate body, responsible for the content and representation of a work". (Buchanan).

Automated software

It is used in a wide variety of tasks and contexts from circulation control, acquisitions, cataloguing to the provision of web services and electronic databases.

Automation

"Automation is the technology of automatic working in which the handling method, the processes and the design of processed material are integrated to utilize as is economically justifiable of mechanization of thought and effort in order to achieve an automatic and in some cases a self-regulating chain of processes" (L. Goodman). The term automation was first introduced by D. S. Harder in 1936. *See* Library Automation.

Auto Web Browser

Auto Web Browser 1.4 of Sekhol Technology is a free browsing / searching tool. It automatically sends requests to major search engines, downloads the pages, filters and analyses them and then surfs further downloading other potentially interesting pages using the links from the meaningful part of the relevant document.

B

BTIS (Biotechnology Information System)

The Biotechnology Information System is a large network of computers established by NIC as distributed information system in India a linking state capitals to the Centre and also districts with cities through satellite communications. The networking of information and communication system thus facilitates the use and sharing of available resources in specialized Centres under BTIS. This network is linked with the NICNET system and every node of BTIS has an identity and they are linked to the satellite communication through a dedicated line. Each node of BTIS operates in conjunction and each computer runs a separate network programme which accepts mail / data files to be sent or received to / from its destination.

Barcodes

These are self-contained machine-readable identification labels with information encoded in a series of black bars and white spaces of varying widths that represent digits and other punctuation symbols. These are readable only by scanner. It is an identification tool that provides an accurate and timely support of the data requirement for sophisticated management systems.

Barcoding in Libraries

This technology offers a lot of comfort and ease of handling bulk routine tasks efficiently. The application of this technology for charging in or out of books in widely accepted and practiced in libraries. With the help of a data gathering device, the barcodes can be used to verify stock at intervals. Misshelving and wrong archiving of books are also auto-detected which helps staff to rectify these challenges.

Objectives: 1. To improve operational efficiency, 2. To save time of users, 3. To achieve accuracy, 4. To reduce operational cost and 5. To make stock verification an easy process.

Barcode Technology

Barcodes are a series of vertical break lines and spaces. The barcode is a simple, compact, graphical way to record data (Wikipedia). They are machine readable. Linear (or one-dimensional or 1 – D) Codes, two dimensional codes (e.g. data matrix) and composite codes (a combination of 1-D or 2 – D symbolizes) are available.

Basic or Simple Subject

"If a work or document contains overall description of an entity or an entity set, which are Central theme of a work, or contains an exposition of a theoretical concept or concepts about some phenomenon / phenomena or thing(s) then the subject of the work is deemed to be of type simple subject" (S. R. Ranganathan) e.g. Algebra, Mathematics, Biology, Botany, Political Science, Literature, Sanskrit literature, etc.

Berlin Declaration (on Open Access)

The Berlin Declaration on Open Access to knowledge in the 'Sciences and Humanities' is a clear commitment to encourage European researchers to change their publishing habits. Signed by Heads of numerous European research Organizations and funding bodies it states that "Our organizations are interested in the further promoting of the new Open Access Paradigm to gain the most benefit for science and society by 2005 in support of Open Access Projects".

The Berne Copyright Convention, 1886

This Convention first established the recognition of Copyrights between sovereign nations and is administered by World Intellectual Property Organization (WIPO) since 1971. It is the oldest Copyright Convention. Presently 179 countries adhere to Berne Convention including the US, Canada, and all European Union (EU) Countries. Berne provides a minimum standard of Copyright protection. Countries which adhere to Berne agreed to include this minimum standard in their own copyright laws. If a person is protected by copyright in his / her own country, then he / she is protected in other 178 countries which adhere to Berne. This convention has been revised few times in the past: Berlin in 1908, Rome in 1928, Brussels in 1948, Stockholm in 1967 and Paris in 1971. (Wikipedia).

Best Practice

1. A best practice is a technique, method, process, activity, incentive or reward that is believed to be more effective at delivering a particular outcome that any other techniques, methods, process, etc.
2. "Quality of high standard, excellence, highly improved, outstanding, par excellence service" (OED).
3. "It is an application of procedures to yield superior results which means way of doing things in particular organization as guidelines for good practices" (UGC-NAAC).

Bibliographic Control (BC)

1. "Mastery over written, published records, which is provided by and for the purpose of bibliography. Bibliographic Control is synonymous with effective access through bibliographies". (UNESCO).
2. Bibliographic Control is "the development and maintenance of a system of adequate recording of all forms of material published and unpublished, printed, non-printed or otherwise, which add to the sum of human knowledge and information" (L. A. Handbook).
3. "The process of identifying and recording in a standardized form the bibliographic data about documents published or available in a given area

(Subject field, country, region or worldwide), and of gathering these bibliographic data so that they can be further used in order to identify and have access to the documents".

Uses: 1. Assists in locating the existence of or identifying a book or other reading materials. 2. Enables to find out a document which has been already published on a particular subject. 3. Avoids duplication in research and publication, 4, Facilitates in book selection, acquisition and processing work. 5. Helps in identification of bibliographical details of a publication. 6. Helps in controlling, sharing and exchanging bibliographical information. 7. Helps in preserving scholarship and culture of a place to future generations, and 8. Helps in furtherance of research.

Bibliographic Coupling

This concept was introduced by Kessler (1963) and demonstrated the existence of the phenomenon and argued for its usefulness as an indicator of subject relatedness. Documents are said to be bibliographically coupled if they share one or more bibliographic references. The number of shared references is directly proportional to the strength of bibliographic coupling.

Bibliographic Instruction

It means to furnish library users with some degree of familiarity with library services and to provide knowledge and skills needed for identification and retrieval of relevant information.

Bibliography

A list of documents containing bibliographic description of documents. E.g. by subject, by author, or by geographical entity, general or specified, selective or exhaustive, current or retrospective and so on.

Bibliographic Organization (BO)

"The Pattern of effective arrangement which results from the systematic listing of the records of human communication" (V. W. Clapp). The two terms Bibliographic Control (BC) Bibliographic Organization (BO) are often used as synonymously.

Bibliographic record

A collection specifically defined character strings, including a record label a directory and bibliographic data describing one or more bibliographic items treated as one entity. It may contain one or more record segments.

Bibliographic record formats

For libraries MARC (Machine Readable Cataloging) is the standard format for storage and exchange of bibliographic records and related information in machine-readable form along with other different formats such as Common Communication Format (CCF), ONIX – the International Book Industry Standards conform to ISO 2709:1996 Information and Documentation - format for Information Exchange.

Bibliographical Services

To organize the explosion of recorded knowledge, Librarians, Document lists and Information Scientists have been bringing various types of bibliographical services for easy location and retrieval of mass of material. The phrase bibliographical services includes abstracting and indexing services, union catalogues, and lists, current awareness services (CAS) forthcoming publication lists, periodical lists, news summaries, translation services and reprographic services.

Bibliographic Standard

It is aimed at achieving consistency and uniformity of practice in the creation of bibliographic records.

Bibliography

1. It is used "to denote the knowledge or study or description of books as physical entities, or as containers of intellectual matter. Briefly bibliography may be said to be the study about books" (A. K. Ohdedar).
2. ".....the systematic study and description of books. Bibliography is either (1) the listing of books according to some system (descriptive or enumerative bibliography) and (2) the study books as tangible objects (Critical or analytical, bibliography...." (The New Encyclopaedia Britannica, Vol.2, 15th ed. 1993).

Bibliometrics

1. It is statistical analysisisof written publications such as books and articles. The most commonly used bibliometric methods are citation analysis and content analysis. Allen Richard first coined the term 'bibliometrics' stating that the definition and purpose of bibliometrics is to shed light on the process of written communications and of the nature and course of a discipline by meaning of counting and analyzing the various facets of written communication.
2. "the use of documents and patterns of publication on which mathematical and statistical methods have been applied" (BSI).
3. "The quantitative treatment of properties of recorded discourse and behavior operating to it" (R. A. Fairthorne)
4. "The Organization, Classification and Quantitative evaluation of publication pattern of all macro micro communication along with their authorship by mathematical and statistical calculus" (Sengupta).

Big Data

1. It is "data that exceeds the processing capacity of conventional database systems. The data is too big,

moves too fast or does not fit the structures of your database architecture. To gain value from this data, you must choose an alternative way to process it" (Ed. Dumbill). Characteristics: 1. Volume, 2. Variety, 3. Velocity, 4. Veracity and 5. Volatility.

2. "Extremely large data sets that may be analyzed computationally to reveal patterns, trends and associations, especially relating to human behavior and interactions" (Oxford dictionaries.com).

Big Data Analytics

It is the process of collecting, organizing and analyzing large sets of data to discover patterns and other useful information. It is useful to find out intelligent decisions to improve operations.

Bioinformatics

Bioinformatics is a discipline where biology, computer science and information technology have merged to form single discipline. The purpose of bioinformatics is to enable the discovery of new biological insights with the help of computers and involves processing of data (collection, analysis, mining, management, integration, simulation and visualization) originated from laboratory experiments.

Biometrics

It is an automated method of identifying a person and verifying the identity of a person based on physiological or behavioral characteristics. Examples of Physiological Characteristics include hand or finger images, facial characteristics and Iris recognition. Behavioral characteristics are traits that are learned or acquired.

Blended learning

Higher educational institutions have started responding by incorporating features of Internet based teaching into their conventional teaching modes as well as in the ODL mode. This pedagogy approach which drws upon the best features of face to face learning, online learning and practices in ODL, is gaining popularity by the name of blended learning.

Blog or Weblog

Blog or Weblog defined by Reichard and Harder as a "Website resembling personal journal that is updated with individual entries or postings". Stone described Weblog as a "Personal Website that provides updated headlines and news articles of other sites that are of interest to the user, also may include journal entries, commentaries and a recommendation compiled by the users". Definitions: 1. Wikipedia defines a blog (a contraction of the term Weblog) as 'a type of website usually maintained by an individual with regular entries of commentary, descriptions of events or other material such as graphics or video. Blog entries are commonly displayed in reverse chronological order". 2. "It is an online journal comprised by links and postings in reverse chronological order meaning the most recent posting appears at the top of the page " (Dan Gilmour). 3. Weblog is an "Online journal – A Web Page with a series of short entries in reverse chronological order". (Darlene Pitcher).

Features : 1. Provide commentary on news on a particular subject, 2. Function as more personal online diaries, 3. A Typical blog combines text, images and links to other blogs, Webpages and other media related to its topic., 4. Postings on a blog are almost and always arranged in chronological order with the most recent additions, 5. Blogs are frequently updated, 6. It has facility for readers to respond immediately.

Types : 1. Personal blogs, 2. Corporate blogs and 3. Question blogs.

Bluetooth

It is a low power, short-range (30 feet) networking specification with moderately fast transmission speeds of 800

Kilobites per second. It provides a wireless, point-to-point, personal area network for PDAs, note books, printers, mobile phones and audio components and other devices.

Book-Bank Facility

It refers to the service offered by the Institute / Library or other Welfare Society to the students in terms of their study books. Mostly college libraries offer this type of facility to their students. Special rules are framed to administer this facility. It is an additional book lending facility for poor / deserving students under which they can borrow books for an academic year. Mostly needy, deserving and economically poor students of a College / Institute are eligible for it.

Boolean Operators

These are also known as logical operators derived its name from British born Irish mathematician George Boole (1815-64) who wrote about a system of logic which can be used to produce better search results by formulation of a precise search statement. From his writing Boolean Operators were derived and these are 'OR', 'AND' and "Not" which are used to link keywords and phrases to formulate a more precise and specific search statement.

Usefulness : these can be very useful for focusing a search to the topic particularly when the topic might contain elements of multiple subjects. These operators also allow one to connect various pieces of information together to find exactly what one is looking for.

Born digital

The term 'born-digital' was coined by Randel Metz, a Web Developer in 1993. "Born-digital resources are items created and managed in digital form" (Ricky Erway). According to Wikipedia "the term born-digital referes to materials that originate in a digital form. This is in contrast to digital reformatting, through which analog material becomes digital. It is most often used in relation to digital libraries and the issues that go along with said organizations such as digital presentation and intellectual property". E.g. Born-digital resources are: *e-Books, e-Journals, Online Databases, e-Newspapers, Websites, etc.*

C

CAB Abstracts

CAB International (Centre for Agriculture and Bioscience International) is an inter-governmental organization registered with the United Nations (UN) with its Headquarters at Wallingford, Oxon (UK). CAB Abstracts is a bibliographic database compiled by CAB International and covers the subjects of agriculture in the broadest sense and in a most comprehensive manner. Journals, monographs, conferences, books, annual reports and other sources from more than 100 countries and in over 70 different languages and scanned regularly for inclusion in the CAB Abstracts database, to produce approximately 1,50,000 new records per year. More than 16,000 serials and other publications are scanned to produce the abstracts.

CALIBNET (Calcutta Library Network)

It was inaugurated on 21st September 1993 by Prof. S. K. Sen, Minister for Power, Government of West Bengal. It was established to serve the collective interest of Calcutta's (Kolkata) institutional libraries by means of computer based library automation and networking, aimed at optimum utilization of bibliographic resources of participating libraries by mechanization of resource sharing and electronic access. The prime objective is to institute systematic inter-library cooperation and document delivery amongst the participating libraries of Kolkata. The participating libraries can stimulate and sustain resource sharing with a view to largely free libraries from stranglehold of financial crunch.

CCF (Common Communication Format)

In April 1978, the UNESCO General Information Programme (UNESCO/PGI) sponsored International Symposium on Bibliographic Exchange Formats which was held in Taormina (Italy) organized by the UNISIST International Centre for Bibliographic Description (UNIBID) in cooperation with others to study the desirability and feasibility of establishing maximum compatibility between existing bibliographic exchange format. As a result of this symposium, resolution passed at the symposium for UNESCO to set up the ad-hoc group for the establishment of CCF

The objective of CCF was stated to provide a detailed and structured method for recording a number of mandatory and optional elements in a computer readable bibliographic record for exchange purpose between two or more computerized systems. It is also useful to single bibliographic agency engaged in structuring its own format simultaneously keeping compatibility with the CCF. The first edition of CCF was published in 1984 and the second edition in 1988. Bibliographic agencies around the world developed national and local formats based on the CCF.

The chief purpose of the format was to provide a detailed and structured method of recording a number of mandatory and optional data elements in a computer-readable bibliographic record for exchange purposes between two or more computer-based systems. The three major purposes are: *1. To permit the exchange of bibliographic records between groups of libraries and abstracting and indexing services, 2. To permit a bibliographic agency to use a single set of computer programs to manipulate bibliographic records received from both libraries and abstracting and indexing services, 3. To serve as basis of a format for any agency's own bibliographic database.*

CCOD (Current Contents on Diskette)

It is an information database for scientific researchers that provide weekly access to latest contents listings from current issues of the most important and leading scientific journals. It is a product of Institute of Scientific Information (ISI), Philadelphia. Through special arrangement with the Journal Publishers, ISI receives journal issues as soon as they are published. These content pages are immediately processed and included in the Current Contents issue.

CD-ROM (Compact Disc-Read only Memory)

CD-ROM introduced in 1985, the audio CD in 1982 is basically an optical disc. It, in the form of CDE-ROM has become increasingly important as a medium storage and dissemination of information during the 1990s. The CD-ROM technology is mainly being used in the area of bibliographic databases. A CD can store 650 megabytes of data that is equal to data of around 550 floppies or 300,000 types pages. Since it can store large volume of structured data-bibliographic, full-text, multimedia and image types, the CD-ROM has brought about a revolution in the information world.

CDS / ISIS

It is the abbreviation of Computerized Documentation Service / Integrated set of Information System. PC based Library Automation Software being in use in Indian Libraries was developed by UNESCO and marketed by Department of Science and Technology, Govt. of India. This was in use until 1995. This did not suit the overall requirements of Indian Libraries. During the early 1990 period library professionals felt the need for comprehensive library software to be developed for libraries in India. This software worked on simple IBM compatible PC / XT and was also available on UNIX and NOUELL Platform.

CSIR Electronic Journals Consortium

This was started in June 2002 after an agreement with Elsevier Science Access to 1200+ electronic journals of Elsevier Science has been enabled to most of the CSIR Labs in India. It is one of the CSIR Networked Projects under Tenth Five Year Plan. This consortium was taken care by NISCAIR (CSIR) one of the labs of the CSIR.

It has been envisaged to provide accessibility to 4500+ electronic journals published by leading publishers and learned institutions and societies. The usage of the e-journals has been steadily increasing. There has been fivefold increase in usage from 5000 downloads in January 2002 to nearly 30,000 downloads in December 2002. The CSIR and its 40 constituent laboratories together subscribe to over 3,356 foreign research journals at a cost about Rs.25 crores every year (R.S. Bisen).

Capacity building

A process to assist and adapt an institution's ability to accomplish its mission. The process involves improving the abilities, skills and expertise of teachers towards enhancing their knowledge and method of teaching. Teachers have to make special effort to give every student as sense of belonging so that the institution provides a positive working and learning environment that is conducive both to student learning and professional academic development.

Career Guidance

It refers to services and activities intended to assist individuals of any age and at any point throughout their lives to make educational, training and occupational choices and to manage their careers. Such service may be found in schools, universities and colleges in training institution in public employment services, in the work places, in the voluntary or community sector and in the private sector (OECD / The European Community, 2004).

Central Science Library (CSL), University of Delhi

It was established in the year 1981. It is housed in three-storied building having a carpet area of 22,595 sft with a sitting capacity of 185 seats. The administration of CSL is under the Dean, Faculty of Science. It has Internet access facility and is meant for science stream clientele only. All internet services like e-mail, browsing and downloading are open to the students and faculty. In some cases printout of articles are also provided. At present more than 90 databases and 28074 online journals from various publishers are available.

Centre on Rural Documentation (CORD)

It was established with a mandate to act as a national documentation centre for rural development information at National Institute of Rural Development (NIRD) now (NIRDPR) i.e. Panchayat Raj at Hyderabad. Over the years CORD has developed a strong database of books, reports, journals articles, etc. It has achieved the distinction of being one of the few social science libraries in the country which have computerized their databases. The computerized databases as in the 2001, consists of nearly 1,50,000 references. In addition to this, CORD acquired CD-ROM databases viz: Ag Econ CD, World Development Reports, UN Databases, Information Dissemination activities of CORD are carried out through different information products like CORD Alerts, CORD Index, Directories, etc.

Change management

It has been described as "crafting a more fluid, focused and adaptive organization so that, no matter what the next big change looks like, your people and processes with continually adjust. And your Company will find new and better ways to work for its customers" (Ranson and Krighton)

Chronopolis Project

This project provides long-term archiving and

preservation services for digital content provided by the California Digital Library and the Inter-University Consortium for Political and Social Sciences (ICPSR). Under this project some core archiving and preservation tools and services have been developed under a framework, popularly called ADAPT - Approach to Digital Archiving and Preservation Technology. The mode is based on a layered digital object architecture which includes a set of modular tools and services built on Open Standards and Web Technologies. The project also borrows from Open Archival Information System (OAIS) Reference Framework.

Citation

"It allows us to acknowledge how the scholarship of others has contributed to our work, to distinguish for our readers which ideas are our own and which are borrowed and to give our readers a path by which they can trace the intellectual development of the ideas we present" (C. Bradley).

Citation Analysis

It is an indirect method to assess the information sources used by various categories of users. It is a worthwhile area of research and refers to references one text to another text with information where that text can be found. It is useful for understanding subject relationships, authorship pattern, impact, publication trends and so on. It is a major area of bibliometric research which uses various method of citation analysis to establish relationships between authors and their works.

It also serves other purposes like: as a bibliography for preparing ranked list of periodicals, for understanding the relative use of different types of documents, to find out the relatedness and dependence of subjects, to calculate the citation rate of journals, to find out impact factor for a concerned journal to calculate the immediacy Index, etc.

Citation Indexing

It is an organized listing of cited articles each of which is accompanied by a list of citing articles identified by a source citation. Eugene Garfield is the founder of Institute of Scientific Information and the Visionary of Citation Indexing and searching for scholarly literature.

Citation Management Tool

"It is any resource, program or service that supports citation management or the understanding, gathering, organization and use of the research and information literacy" (D. Childress).

CLOCKSS

The CLOCKSS (Controlled Lots of Copies Keep Stuff Safe) is a not-for-profit joint venture started by libraries and publishers to ensure long term access to scholarly publications in digital format. At present there are 164 libraries and publishers who have entrusted their content to CLOCKSS for long term preservation. It is unique because it commits to make all content from the archive freely available to the world after a trigger event has happened.

Clearing House

This has come into being as a hybrid information service. It acts as a switching operation, providing access through referral to appropriate resources or serving as a collecting agency for special types of documentation in order to redistribute them upon request. Union Catalogues and lists are compiled for this specific purpose. Example: SENDOC (Small Enterprises National Documentation Centre) at Hyderabad is a best example of clearing house. It provides varied information on small industries. Its work is organized into six functions such as: library, documentation, audio-visual publications, organizational communications and data processing.

Clinical Information Resources

These are information resources which provide support to evidence-based practice for the patient care provided by physical / medical practicenors. It is a platform for faculty and students to access many online clinical databases like e-books, e-journals and other electronic information resources and services.

Clinical Medical Librarianship

It is a specialized service originated in the early 70s, popularly called as clinical medical librarianship and was first introduced by Lambat University of Missouri-Kansas City Medical Library and MLA.

Cloud Computing

1. It is a style of computing in which massively scalable and elastic IT Enabled capabilities are delivered as a service to external customers using internet technologies (Christy and Carina).

2. It can be defined as "simply the sharing and use of applications and resources of a network environment to get work done withut concern about ownership and management of the network resources and applications" (Mark&Shane E. Scale).

3. It is a new technology which is an improvement and distributed computing, parallel computing and grid computing.

The basic principle of cloud computing is making tasks distributed among large number of computers but not in local computers or remote servers (R. Sanchati and G. Kulkarni).

Cloud Computing: Characteristics and Advantages

Some of the important characteristics are:

(a) Versatility, (b) Co-effectiveness, (c) Virtualization, (d) Security, (e) Sustainability, (f) Scalability, (g) User-friendly, (h)

Resource optimization, (i) Infrastructure and service-level agreements (P.Y.Thomas and F. H. CervVone)

Advantages: Some important advantage from the point of view of a library are: *(a) No need to own all infrastructure facilities, (b) Provides large amounts of processing Power, (c) can be used as a personal workspace, d) Since it is not location specific, it provides opportunity for ubiquitous computing, (e) Capital expenditure minimized, (f) far more economic as payment is based on utilization of service, (g) No need to copy all stuff from one PC to another when buying a new one, (h) A Convenient tool to engage in scholarship of teaching and learning (D. Hamilton, V. Aggarwal).*

Cloud Computing: Infrastructure

It resides in a large data centre managed by service providers who offer computing resources anywhere, any time at an economically affordable cost i.e. pay-as-you go basis (A. M. Sharif). According Eric Hand "In Cloud computing not just the data but the software also resides within cloud and one can access everything not only throughout PCs but also cloud-friendly devices such as smart phones, PDAS, the Mega Computers (Super Computers) enabled by Virtualization and software as a service".

Co-citation Analysis

It is a unique method used for studying the cognitive structure of science and assessing the research productivity. It is a research tool for examining the intellectual development and structure of the scientific discipline. It is based on grouping together the papers that are frequently cited in pairs.

Collaborative or Collective or Group blog

It is usually written by a group of people blog on a specific topic such as Meta Filters. It can be either open to the Public or limited a specific community.

Collaborative Research (CR)

It is "a process of functional interdependence between scholars in their attempt to coordinate skills, tools and rewards" (Narsi Patel).

Collection Development

1. It covers a broad range of activities related policies and Procedures of selection, Assessing user needs, evaluation of the present collection, weeding out, strong parts of the collection and planning for resource sharing. Collection development is not any single activity or group of activities; it is planning and decision making process. Criteria for collection developments: *1. Information explosion, 2) Inter-disciplinary nature of studies and demands for information, 3. Increase rate of obsolescence, 4. Multiple forms of data availability, and 5. Lack of adequate ways of retrieval of nascent information.*

Evaluation: Measures considered for evaluation: *1. Size of the collection, size of rare collection, size of subject, date, language, 2. Number of volumes per user, number of volumes per document circulated current growth rate, 3. Amount of collection used and 4. Expenditure on collection. Constraints in collection development: 1. Cost of publications, 2. Space limitation, 3. Manpower Limitation.*

2. The process of panning a stock acquisition program not simply to cater for immediate needs, but to build a content and reliable collection over a number of years to meet the objectives of the service". (Harrod's Glossary)

3. "A process of making certain the information needs of the people using the collection are met in a timely and economic manner using information resources produced both inside and outside the organization" (R.F. Munn).

Collection Development Policy (CDP)

It is a set of theoretical goals or statement of actual practice. It can act as a guiding point in various activities related planning, budgeting, selecting and acquiring of library documents.

College library

Functions : 1. Provides reference material required for supplementary class-room instruction. Such materials include reference books, journals, pamphlets, films, slides, digital resources, etc. 2. Provides technical and specialized study material needed to keep the faculty abreast of their fields for teaching, research and publication purposes, 3. Provides the material needed by research scholars and faculty members. 4. Encourages students to refer books and other reading material independently as a means of acquisition of new knowledge, 5. Provides study material needed for extension and distance learners in colleges where distance learning programmes are offered.

Commitment

"A strong belief in the acceptance of organizational goals and values, willingness to exert efforts towards organizational goal accomplishment and strong desire to maintain organizational membership" (L. W. Poster).

Communication

1. "It is the sum of all the things one person does when he wants to create understanding in the mind of another. It involves systematic and continuous process of telling, listening and understanding" (Louis A. Allen).
2. "Communication is the ability of various functional grouping within the enterprise to understand each other's functions and concerns" (Peter Drucker).
3. "Communication is essentially a social phenomenon, because of its importance to the structure, organization and behavior of the society as well as character of the individual". (J. Shera).

Community Information (CI)

1. "Any geographical community or neighborhood will be

made up of a number of communities, defined by race, social class or income group, employment, leisure interest, religion and so on, each with its own informal information network that has group without the help of librarians or any other information advice workers" (Bob Usherwood).

2. "CI is considered to be that information required by members of the public (or those acting on their behalf) to make effective use of the resources potentially available to them in the communities in which they live. Such information may be needed to help solve problems in the fields of housing, disability, household finance, marriage, employment and so on" (Michael Edwards).

Components : (1) Local information such as calendar of local events, courses and other educational and employment opportunities and basic information such as those concerning government agencies, local organizations, clubs, etc., (2) Trans local information such as information useful to the community pertaining to localities beyond local area or community concerned, (3) Public Policy information such as health and hygiene, environment, conservation of energy and resources, agriculture, animal husbandry, useful arts and fine arts, technology as well as political and socio-economic awareness.

Community Information Centre (CIC)

It is defined "as a centre which assists individuals for problem solving and participation in the democratic process. The services concentrate on the needs of those who do not have ready access to the other sources ofr assistance and on the most important problems that people have to face, problems to do with their homes, their jobs and their rights". (Library Association, UK).

Community Information Policy

Objectives : 1. To identify the information needs of

society based on societal goals and collective approaches to solving problems, 2. To identify priorities and promote publications on variety of media and the information needed by society, 3. To identify, access, collect good publications needed for community service to promote a balance in societal organization and progress, 4. To identify, adopted and utilize variety of information storage and retrieval techniques to better and quicker access to information that is relevant to a seeker, and 5. To identify priorities and promote research in different fields of knowledge that can help to promote the role of public libraries to meet the changing societal aspects as mentioned in 1 to 4 (M.A. Gopinath).

Community Information Service (CIS)

"Services which assist individuals and groups with daily problem-solving and with participation in the democratic process. , The services concentrate on the needs of those who do not have ready access to other sources of assistance and on the most important problems that people have to face problems to do with their homes, their jobs and their rights". (The Library Association, London).

Community Library

A Community library usually a branch library (BL) intended to provide an advice centre and local information for the whole community, rather than only offering book collections to readers.

Complex Subject

"If in a document or a work deals with or contains description of interrelationship, comparison, etc. among two or more basic subjects or compound then such subject of the work or document is deemed to be of type of complex subject". (S. R. Ranganathan) e.g. Influence of Weather on Agriculture, Comparison of Philosophy and Religion, influence of Politics on Education, etc.

Compound Subject

"If in a work or a document, one describes only part or portion of the personality of an entity or an entity set or gives description of one or attributes possessed by entity or entities and some or actions on it by or through other entities in a particular space and time context, then the subject of the work is deemed to be of type compound subject". (S. R. Ranganathan). Eg., Mining of Gold; Botanical Study of Flowers; Foreign Policy of India;Constitution of India; and Telugu Poetry.

Computer literacy

The knowledge and ability to use computers and related technology efficiently with a range of skills covering levels from elementary use to programming and advanced problem solving.

Computer Readable Database (CRDB)

A Computer Readable Database is an organized collection of information in computer readable form. CRDB's may be categorized on the basis of several characteristics: 1. On the basis of the types of data elements forming records of file, Bibliographic e.g. MARC-II database, 2. On the basis of status of the producing agency. Produced by Government Agencies e.g. MEDLARS, 3. On the basis of the subject matter covered by the CRBDS's – Discipline Oriented e.g. C. A. Condensate.

Conflict Management

It refers to the long-term management of intractable conflicts. It is the label for a variety of ways by which people handle grievances – standing up for what they consider to right and against what they consider to be wrong.

Consortium / Consortia

1. It is a cooperative arrangement among groups or institutions or an association or society.

2. "A group of organizations whose purpose is collectively facilitate and support the work of a service programme in ways that add material and human resources beyond those available to each organization individually.

Objectives: 1. Increases the cost benefit per subscription, 2. Prmote rational use of meager resources, 3. Ensures continuous subscription to periodicals subscribed, 4. Develop technical capabilities of the staff operating and use of electronic databases, 5. Reduced information cost, 6. Improved resources sharing.

Need for Consortia : 1. Literature explosion, 2. Limited Resources, 3. Diverse demands of users, 4. Increase in the availability of information in electronic form, 5. Cost saving from library budgets, 6. Increased access to varied information resources in the electronic form.

Advantages : 1. Access to wide range of electronic resources at reasonable cost, 2. Optimum utilization of funds, 3. Opportunity to build up digital libraries, 4. Better Library Services like CAS and SDI, 5. Cost sharing among libraries, 6. Labour and time saving, 7. More services to user community and 8. Effective document delivery system.

Disadvantages : 1. Absence of Journals in Print media, 2. Staff Training required to handle electronic media, 3. High initial investment to realize consortia, 4. Copyright problems, 5. Un-reliable telecommunication links and insufficient bandwidth, 6. Lack of archiving and back files facility and 7, Internet access is necessary (See also Library Consortia).

Content

"Content is just about anything that isn't executable". It could be anything digital that is anything that could be distributed or accessed electronically – that is not software 'This sort of content could be images, audio files, movies and text" (WWW).

Content Analysis (CA)

It is a methodology for studying the content of communication. It analyses in depth using quantitative and qualitative technique of messages using scientific method. It is a research tool use to know the trend of a work.

Purpose: 1. It provides trend of a research work, 2. It provides the area of development, 3. It provides a comparative study of communication, 4. It provides scientific shape of unorganized data, 5. It provides pattern of communication, 6. It provides the flow of information and 7. It saves the time of users.

Content Management

It is effectively collecting, managing and making information available in targeted publication. This is better understood if the context in which the concept of content management is known.

Continuing Education Programme (CEP)

Objectives : 1. To keep abreast and update with the new developments, 2. To develop and maintain competency, 3. To widen experience and practical knowledge, 4. To promote personal job satisfaction and to enhance existing qualifications, 5. To continue his study of basic disciplines which support his profession, 6. To help them in improving career prospects, 7. To meet the challenges of the changing needs and requirements, 8. To learn in implementing new ideas, methods and techniques, 9. To improve effectively teaching methods and programmes and 10. To grow as a person as well as a professional.

Continuing Professional Educational (CPE)

It is continuous process of learning which begins on completion of formal education and continues lifelong. C. O. Houle states that "when the young professional moves into the field, the prime responsibility for his learning passes from the professional school to him and to the association to which he belongs". He faces the needs such as: 1. To keep up with the new knowledge related to his profession, 2. To establish mastering over the new conception of his own profession, 3. To continue his study of basic disciplines which support his profession and 4. To grow as a person as well as a professional.

Cooperative Collection Development (CCD)

CCD marks a total shift in the traditional library philosophy – from the philosophy of possession that libraries worldwide have adhered to for a long past to the current philosophy of providing access to the information through a sharing mechanism be it manual or mechanical. It calls for shared acquisitions, shared use and is a major factor for successful implementation of any resources sharing programme.

Copy Cataloguing

It means "Copying the bibliographical details that is already made available by someone through copy cataloguing facility. It allows libraries to enter all the details of the document without actually typing, thus without much time, money and efforts".

Benefits : *1. No need to type the bibliographic record on the part of the cataloguer. 2. Offers fewer opportunities to commit typographical errors since the whole record are copied, 3. Copied data is more up-to-date and scientific as it is imported from authentic source, 4. Creates uniqueness in creation of bibliographic record, and 5.Promotes resource sharing. (Vishal Bapte).*

Copyright

1. It is a kind of intellectual property right. Generally it understood as a legal right. This right is provided by the laws of a country to the authors for the protection of their original works of authorship. It ensures certain minimum safeguards of the rights of authors over their creations.

2. A set of exclusive rights granted to the author or creator or an original work including right to copy, distribute and adapt the work.
3. "The exclusive right given by law, for a certain term of years to an author, composer, etc., or his assignee to print, publish or sell copies of his original work" (OED).

Corporate blog

It is for employees of corporations to post their official or semi-official blogs about their work. This type of weblogs could be a disastrous if bloggers do not handle them carefully.

Corporate Social Responsibility (CSR)

"A concept that an enterprise is accountable for its impact on relevant stake holders. It is a continuous commitment by business to behave fairly and responsibility and contribute to economic development while improving the quality of life of the work force and their families as well as local community and the society at large" (European Union). In broader terms CSR means a collection of policies, programs and practices evolved, adopted and followed by a company that is based on certain values, including respect for people, concern for the communities and care for environment.

Cost Benefit Analysis

"Cost Benefit Analysis as a technique designed to determine the feasibility of a project or plan by quantifying its cost and benefit" (Web Definition).

Cryptography

It is the science and art of secret writing. It dates back to the period of ancient Greece. It is a discipline that embodies the principles, means and methods for transforming data in order to hide its information contents, prevents undetected modification and prevents its unauthorized users.

Cyber Crime

It is an unlawful activity in cyberspace brought about by computer experts and they constitute of hackers, crackers, disgruntled employees. Cyber crimes can be generated from Digital Library, Cyber Café, Computer Lab and Office or even from home PC where Internet Connections are available. These crimes can be committed against person, property, corporate bodies and Governments.

Cybermetrics

It is "the study of the quantitative aspects of construction and use of information resources, structures and technologies on the whole Internet, drawing on bibliometrics and informatrics approaches" (Bjorneborn and Ingwersen).

It is a branch of knowledge which employs mathematical and statistical techniques to quantify web sites or their components and concepts, measuring their growth, stability, propagation and use, examines the authenticity of the content, established laws governing these factors, studies, the efficiency of cyber information systems, services, products and assesses the impact of cyber age on society.

Cyber Social Work

It is the utilization of Internet technology to enhance social work practice. This enhanced practice includes the use of web pages, listservs, E-mail, Chat-rooms, search engines and other interactive web based technologies to communicate with clients and colleagues, gather and disseminate information related to social work practice, engage in social and political advocacy and to advance the social work profession nationally and internationally.

Cyber Space

The word Cyber traces its origin from the concept of cyber space which means virtual space or the apparent location within which the electronic activities occur. The aggregation of internet, intranets and the World Wide Web (WWW) is dubbed as Cyber Space.

Cyber-Terrorism

1. "Cyber-terrorism is the use of computers and information technology, particularly internet to cause harm of severe disruption with the advancing political goals".

2. Cyber-terrorism is premeditated politically motivated attack against information, computer system programs and data which results in violence against the noncombatant targets by the sub-national groups or the clandestine agents" (Wikipedia).

Cybrarian (Person)

1. "A Librarian who can maneuver through Cyberspace with ease, plucking information from its farthest reaches". The term was coined by library legend, Michel Bauwens which considers the implications of the digital revolution.

2. A Cybrarian can be defined as an Information Specialist who deals with more of web content in order to reach his targeted user group. He always updates his knowledge of information resources, information handling tools and the fast changing needs of users as a result of network revolution or web revolution.

Cybrarian (Software)

It is web based seamless and fully integrated Library Management Software System hosted on Remote server. This is based on SaaS (Software as a Service) Concept where users have to pay-as-you-use basis. SaaS is a new model for delivery software over internet. It is a shift from Packaged Software to Software as a service (SaaS). In this model, the user is saved from the hassles of buying licensed copies of software like OS, R / DBMS, Application Software, Anti-Virus, etc.

D

DCMI (Dublin Core Matadata Initiative)

This is an organization dedicated to promoting the wide spread adoption of interoperable metadata standards and developing specialized metadata vocabularies for describing resources that enable more intelligent information discovery systems. The mission of DCMI is to make easier to find resources using Internet through the following activities:

1. Developing metadata standards for discovery across domains,
2. Defining frameworks for the inter-operation of metadata sets and
3. Facilitating the development of community or disciplinary specific metadata sets that are consistent with Items 1 and 2.

DELNET (Delhi Library Network)

This Network was launched in January 1988 at the India International Centre, New Delhi. It is the first operational library network in India. Sponsored by the National Information System for Science and Technology (NISSAT), Department of Science and Technology, Government of India, it was started as Project of India International Centre in 1988 and later officially registered as a Society in June 1992. The main objectives of DELNET are to promote sharing of resources among the libraries by developing a Network of Libraries, storing and disseminating information services to users and to coordinate efforts of suitable collection development and reducing unnecessary duplication wherever possible

DeLCON

To meet the growing R & D in formation requirements of Department of Biotechnology (DBT) Institutions,

Government of India, the DBT's Electronic Library Consortium (DeLCON) was launched in January 2009. It was national initiative for providing access to scholarly electronic resources including full-text and bibliographic databases in all the life sciences subject disciplines to DBT Institutions in the Country.

Objectives (briefly): 1. To provide access to high quality and scholarly electronic resources to DBT Institutions, 2. To promote interaction and inter-library cooperation amongst the participating members, 3. To bring qualitative change in teaching, learning and research, 4. To increase the research productivity of the institujtions, 5. To provide quick and efficient access to scholarly content, 6. To extend the benefit of consortium to its associate members, 7. To impart training to users, librarians and research scholars and faculty members, 8. To promote use of e-resources with gradual decrease in print subscriptions.

DESIDOC (The Defense Scientific Information and Documentation Centre)

DESIDOC is one of the DRDO (Defense Research and Development Organization) Laboratories which is meant for collecting and disseminating S & T Information of interest and relevant to DRDO Scientists and Technologists. It started functioning in 1958 and it was then known as Scientific Information Bureau (SIB). As the activities of DRDO increased and expanded, the activities of DESIDO also increased. In 1967 SIB was renamed as DESIDOC. Divisions: 1. Defense Science Library (DSL), 2. Information Services Division, 3. DRDO Publications, 4. Human Resource Development, 5. Technical Services and 6. R & D Unit.

DEVINSA (Development information Network for South Asia)

This network was started in 1986 with financial support from IDRC, Canada. The main objective of this network was to organize a computerized database on socio-economic development in South Asia containing data primarily about non-conventional material like research project reports, doctoral theses, working papers, etc, and share this development information between academia, policy makers, etc., so as to contribute to the socio-economic development of the region. It is coordinated at the Marga Institute, Sri Lanka and the other Members of the Network are Bangladesh, India, Male, Nepal and Pakistan. It has been found to be very useful by research policy makers and organizations engaged in developmental studies.

DOAG

The Directory of Open Access Journals (DOAJ) is a website of online Directory maintained by Lund University libraries, Sweden which includes quality open access journals around the world. The resources are catalogued at the journal titles level and the directory also attempts to obtain article metadata from the journal owner to make article level content searchable in the system. The journal directory aims to cover all open access scientific and scholarly journals that use a quality control system to guarantee the content. The aim of DOAJ is also to increase the visibility and ease of use of open access scientific and scholarly journals and thereby promoting their increased usage and impact.

DTP (Desk Top Publishing)

This is currently the most popular application of PC's which has brought the entire printing press on to one's desktop. One can create photo ready documents and thus do away with manual typesetting and composing which takes many man hours. One can print books, manuals, brochures, bulletins using specialized DTP Software on all kinds of printers. The software pages available for DTP are sophisticated to produce different type styles of text, integrate graphics with text and prepare documents in such a manner that one can actually see them on the screen before sending them for printing.

DVD

It stands for Digital Video Disc or Digital Versatile Disc. It looks just like a CD but has a bigger data storage capacity. Like a CD, data is recorded on DVD in a spiral trail of tiny pits and the discs are read using a laser beam. The DVD's larger capacity is achieved by making the pits smaller and the spiral tighter, and by recording the data in as many as four layers, two on each side of the disc.

D-Space

D-Space is new open digital repository system from the MIT and Hewlett-Packard Labs designed to support digital collections of academic research institutions, as well as the SPARC conception of institutional repositories for the digital research materials. The system is duly featured, digital asset management system including a submission system that support complex, flexible workflows, as well as a limited support for access control and delivering complex digital contents.

Key features : 1. It is open source software distributed under GPL, 2. It has very good multilingual support and it is platform independent, 3. Software is written in JAVA and the system runs Tomcat JSP Service, 4. D-space repository can be divided into communities, 5. Community, collection and item have persistent identifiers called handles, 6. Items can be described according to Dublin Core elements, 7. D-space provides authorization. Each user of D-space should have authorization he/she wishes to upload a document, 8. D-space requires mail server for posting automatically generated mails regarding activities for authorized person, 9. Workflow can be defined within the D-space and persons can be authorized to submit, edit and view, and 10. Searching is done in D-space according to meta-data submitted but it also supports full-text search.

D-Space@INFLIBNET

INFLIBNET Centre at Ahmadabad has been maintaining an institutional repository on D-Space. This institutional repository contains articles published in the proceedings of the International and National Conferences and Seminars organized by the Centre. It also includes news and other important material related to library and information science areas.

Data

1. "Numerical or Quantitative Values derived from Scientific Experiments" (McGraw-hill Encyclopedia of Science and Technology). 2. "Data is piece of non-discursive information" (Bhattacharya). It includes any facts, figures, letters, symbols, words, charts, maps or graphs that represent an idea, object, condition or situation.

Characteristics : UNIDO has listed the following characteristics: availability, compatibility, reliability, flexibility, timeliness, processibility, sensitivity and cost benefit. Categories of data – 1. Data with reference time factor, 2. Location factor, 3. Mode of generation, 4. Nature of quantitative values, 5. Terms of expression and 6. Mode of Presentation.

Databank

1. Information facility which collects data eventually in machine readable form, often from various sources and provide access to them.
2. OECD defines Databank as "an information system for utilizing data from a variability of sources by integrating data into consistent sets, thereby facilitating access, manipulations and correlations of the data for a group of potential users".

Database

1. It is a computerized collection of logically related set of data or records about something that are stored and organized in a computer.
2. It means subject oriented data gathered and maintained in a server by an official entity, displaying a highly interactivity with the user as well as search engine capability, data records file, query or sales transactions, product catalogues, etc.
3. It is an "Organized set of machine readable records containing bibliographic or document related data" (M.E. Williams).

Types of databases : 1. Bibliographic databases, 2. Full-text databases, 3. Directory databases,

Quality Criteria : 1. Consistency, 2. Coverage / Scope, 3. Timeliness, and 4. Accuracy.

Database Management System (DBMS)

A database management system is composed of a set of programs that create, modify, store, manage, protect and provide access to the database and enable the end users to retrieve information in a variety of ways (C.J. Dates).

Benefits : 1. Different users can share the data stored in the database files and all the information requirements of different users are met. 2. A common and controlled approach is used for adding or inserting new data and deleting, correcting, modifying and retrieving existing data records or portion of it within a database and 3. Users and applications that access data need not be aware of the detailed storage structure of the data on a computer storage device.

Data Centre

A data centre is an organization handling raw or partially processed data or partially processed results. It is often concerned with large-scale phenomena such as census type data on people, goods and materials. *Function:* 1. Data evaluation and compilation service, 2. Data dissemination service, 3. Referral service.

Data Communication System

It links input / output devices at remote locations with one or more central processors. An interface element called modem (modulation-demodulation device) converts the digital into analog signals that can be transmitted through voice communication lines. When two computers are inter connected using telephone lines there will be modems at both ends.

Data literacy

1. It focuses on understanding how to find and evaluate, giving emphasis to the version of the given dataset and the person responsible for it and does not neglect the questions of citing and ethical use of data (ACRL).
2. Specific skills set acknowledge base, which empowers individuals to transform data into information and into actionable knowledge by enabling them to access, interpret, critically assess manage and ethically use data (Kot lay).

Data Mining

1. It is the process of discovering meaningful correlation, patterns or trends by shifting through large amounts of stored data using pattern recognition technologies as well as statistical and mathematical techniques. This would save direct bearing on the reaction times in peace and war.
2. "The automatic extraction of useful, often previously unknown information from large databases or data sets".
3. "The process of exploration and analysis by automatic

or semi-automatic means of large quantities of data to discover meaningful patterns and rules".

Data-PASS

Data-PASS(Data Preservation Alliance for the Social Sciences) is a project supported by NDIIFP of Five Major US Social Science Data Archives. It ensures that all at risk social science data are identified, acquired, archived and preserved for future.

Decision making

It deals with a set of alternative states of nature (outcome, results), a set of alternative reactions that are available to the decision maker, a relation indicating the state or outcome to be expected from each alternative action, and, finally a utility or objective function which orders the outcomes according to their desirability. Ofstad defined decision making "as making a judgment regarding what one ought to do in certain situation after having deliberated on some alternative courses of action".

Delivery of Books (Public Libraries) Act, 1954

The Government of India in the year 1954 enacted the Delivery of Books (Public Libraries) Act, 1954. The Act made it obligatory on the part of every publisher in India to deposit, free of cost, a copy of publication with the National Library (Calcutta) and three other public libraries within 30 days from the date of issue of the publication. The Act was amended in 1956 so as to include newspapers. The other three deposit libraries are: 1. Connemera Public Library, Madras (now Chennai), 2. The Central Library, Town Hall, Bombay (now Mumbai) and 3. Delhi Public Library, Delhi.

Digital Content

It generally refers to the electronic delivery of fiction which is shorter than book-length, non-fiction, documents and other written works of shorter length. Publishers of digital content deliver shorter sized works to the consumer via download to handheld and other wireless devices.

Digital Learning Environment (DLE)

A technical solution for supporting learning, teaching and studying activities. It can be educational software, a digital learning tool, an online study programme or a learning resource. Thus, it consists of a combination of different technical solutions.

Digital Divide
1. It is the gap between those who have access to knowledge, information, ideas and works of information through technology and those who do not. It is the gap between those with access to a wide range of information sources and those who do not. In the global digital information age those who are either unable to access the Internet and the World Wide Web through the application of ICTs and are increasingly disadvantaged in their access to information.
2. It refers to the gap between the people with effective access to digital and information technology and those without. It includes the imbalances in physical access to technology as well as the imbalances in resources and skills needed to effectively participate as 'digital citizen' or 'netizen'. Many believe Andy Grove first coined the term. Some others say the credit goes to Larry Irvin for coining the term.

Implications : 1. Gap between who use computer / internet and those who do not; 2. Gap between broadband network access and usages; 3. Unequal access to computer hardware; 4. Imbalances in the ability to use IT and 5. Gap between literate and illiterate.

Different forms of digital devide : 1. *Social factors:* a) Language divide; b) Gender divide; c) Generation gap; d) E-information literacy 2. *Economic Factors:* a) Economic divide; b) Rural-Urban divide; c) Over-production of documents; 3. Technological divide; 4. Governments policies.

Digital Library

1. It is a structured collection of digital content like text, video or audio developed and made available con the web to meet the information needs of end users. These have great prospective as they can offer a wide range of benefits to researchers, academicians, institutions and learners worldwide (I.H. Witten, D. Bainbridge and D. M. Nichols).

2. C. L. Borgmn defined digital libraries as "Electronic libraries in which large number of geographically distributed users can access contents of large and diverse repositories of electronic objects. Electronic objects include networked text, image, maps, sound videos and catalogues and scientific, business and government data sets".

3. "A digital library is a managed collection of information with associated services by which information is stored in digital formats and accessible over a network" (Arms).

Characteristics: 1. Counterparts of traditional libraries and include both electronic as well as print and multimedia resources such as audio, video, graphics, animation, etc. 2. May also provide access to digital material and resources from outside the actual confines of any one digital library, 3. Support quick and efficient access to a large number of distributed but interlinked information sources that are seamlessly integrated, 4. Include all the process and services offered by traditional libraries.

Need: 1. To keep pace with changing environment of technological innovations, 2. To save valuable shelf space,, 3. To preserve rare and valuable information, 4. To increase the efficiency and effectiveness of a library, 5. To provide faster services and enable multi user access.

Technological Requirements : 1. Computer with high speed processor, sufficient memory and hard-disk space and multi-media configuration, 2. Large flatbed high resolution scanner and digital cameras, 3. Backup facility and devices to take backup of all files, 4. Optical Character Recognition (OCR), 5. ImageeLearning Software, 6.High-speed internet connectivity and 7. Digital Library Software for organizing digital resources.

Digital Library of India

It is the biggest national level digital library initiative in India. It is part of the Universal Digital Library Project, envisaged by Carnegie Mellon University, USA which has some other international partners such as China and Egypt. DLI is coordinated by Indian Institute of Science, Bangalore and is supported by the Ministry of Communication and Information Technology, Government of India. The prime objective is to create a portal for the Digital Library of India which — — foster and free access to all human knowledge and cater to the needs of the Generation of users.

Digital Mobile Library

The Government of India in collaboration with the Centre for Advanced Computing (C-DAC) based in Pune aims the target to bring about one million digital books to the door steps of common people. For spreading and promoting literacy the Internet has facilitated in the Mobile Digital Library. Mobile Van with satellite connection for Internet Connectivity is used. The Van is also equipped with printer and binding machine for providing bound books to the end user from a single point.

Digital object

A digital object is a fundamental unit of the digital library architecture. Digital object has five major components as per a network environment is concerned. These are key metadata and content (bits). The key metadata are of four types viz. handle, properties, transaction log and signature.

Digital Object Identifier (DOI)

It is a system for persistent identification and inter operable exchange of intellectual property on digital networks. It provides an extensible framework for managing intellectual content in any form, at any level of granularity and in any digital environment. DOIs might be used to identify any intellectual property entity, including those already identified by systems such as ISBN and can be used in compatibility with ISBN.

Digital Preservation

It is a process of preserving both digitized and born-digital contents to a distant future in reasonable condition to for access by its users. It involves a set of systematic guidelines, processes, strategies, technology and approaches. The technological obsolesce shorter and uncertain life-period for current storage media, information glut and internet revolution are some of major factors which have make preservation of digital information more complex and challenging.

Definitions : 1. "The process and activities which stabilize and protect reformatted and digital authentic electronic records in forms which are retrievable, readable and usable overtime" (UNESCO). 2. It is a set of procedures, activities and instruments that help to safeguard digital memory overtime. This means to preserve all documents both born-digital and converted to digital, in the long term, preserving their content.

Objectives : 1. To reduce the effect of deteriorating factors such as temperature, light, humidity, flood, fire, fungus, insects, pollution, dust, etc. 2. To maintain and preserve historical value of information, 3. To make information sustain and survive longer. 4. To make it easy to use and handle, 5. To provide wider accessibility, 6. To make information survive longer period.

Advantages : 1. Space saving, 2. Easy access, 3. Easy to handle, 4. Easy to transmit, 5. Saves time, 6. Low cost, 7. Involvement of less manpower.

Disadvantages : 1. Installation process is costly and complex, 2. Lack of infrastructure, 3. Insufficient budget, 4. Shortage of storage expertise especially in India.

Digital Reference Services

These refer to "a network of expertise, intermediation and resources put at the disposal of a user seeking answers in an online / networked environment. A digital reference occurs when a question is received electronically and responded electronically" (McClare Bertot and Ryan). A digital reference generally comprise the following elements viz: 1. The user of the service, 2. The interface (e-mail, web form, chat, video conference, etc.), 3. The information professional, and 4. Electronic resources (including electronic or CD based resources, web resources; local digitized material, etc. as well as print resources (Berube, 2003).

Digital Repository

It is a storage medium where wide range of digital information are stores and disseminate to the user via computer. In an academic library digital repository is an Institutional Repository, where institutions books, papers, theses, question papers, journals and other works are preserved.

Types: 1. In-house repository, 2. Open access repository.

Importance : 1. Useful for engineering institutions and other technical institutions, 2. Provides awareness among he institutions, 3. Connecting link between different departments, 4. Preserves all the contents of an institution and easily retrievable, and 5. Helpful to researchers to prepare a research project.

Digital Resources

The resources which are published in digital format and read by a computer are digital resources. These usually consist of e-books, online journals, online databases, e-thesis and e-dissertation, CD-ROMs, etc. The resources which are available online in digital formats are called digital resources. These resources can be used by users through online access.

Digital resource collection management

It is a systematic and organized approach that allows the management of digital resource to focus on achievable objectives and to attain the best possible results to increase the organizational digital library performance to achieve organization goal.

Digital resource management strategies

1. Users service through greater access to accurate digital information sources;
2. Enhanced information resources and knowledge satisfaction among users.
3. More economical and safer means of storing and keeping track of digital information resources.
4. Easier access to digital information resources like old reports, e-journals, e-books, on-line databases and even audio-visual material, etc.
5. Greater liability and lucidity in operations by monitoring.
6. Improved efficiency and effectiveness in administration and management of digital resources as it has unprecedented access to real-time information.
7. More consistent safety for susceptible and secret information.

8. Appropriate knowledge-based action and intervention can now take place in a timely manner.
9. Library networking through web-based architecture (K. Sarojadevi *et al*)

Digital signature

It means authentication of any electronic record by a subscriber by means of an electronic method or procedure in accordance with the provisions of section 3 of Information Technology Act, 2000.

Digital Watermarking

It is the process of possible embedding information into a digital signal. The signal may be audio, pictures or video for example. If the signal is copied then the information is also carried in the copy. Applications: Can be used for wide range of applications such as: a) Copyright Protection, b) Finger Printing and c) Broadcast monitoring, d) Covert communication (Steganography).

Digitization

1. It refers to "transforming data, information, knowledge of physical objects from various media into digital object" (web definition).
2. It means "acquiring, converting, storing and providing information in a computer format that is standardized, organized and available on demand from common systems. Digitization of assets can include customer information, marketing communication assets (images, video and audio files) and production information, as well as pricing information, inventory / order status and many other application".

Advantages : 1. Increasing access, 2. Preservation, 3. Democratization and 4. Feasibility.

Directory blog

It collects and categories numerous websites with interesting content in an easy to use and constantly updated format. Political blogs also fall into this category.

Directory of Open Access Books (DOAB)

This is a service to provide open access on monographs. It provides a searchable index with links to full text of the publications at the publishers' website or repository for peer-reviewed monographs through open access business model. It invites academic publishers to provide the metadata of their open access books to DOAB.

Directory of Open Access Journals (DOAJ)

It aims to be comprehensive covering all open access (OA) scientific and scholarly journals that use an appropriate quality control system. It is not limited to a particular language or subject areas. There are 3703 journals in the Directory. Currently 1276 journals are searchable at article level. As of today 213723 articles are included in the DOAJ service. The DOAJ is hosted, maintained and partly funded by Lund University Libraries Head Office.

Distance Education (DE)

"A learning system where the teaching behaviors are separated from learning behaviors. The learner works alone or in a group guided by study material arranged by instructor, who together with the tutors, is in a location apart from the students, who however has the opportunity to communicate with tutors with the aid of one or more media such as correspondence, telephone, television and radio. Distance education may be confined to various forms of face-to-face meetings" (M. G. Moore).

Characteristics: 1. Separation of educators and learners, 2. Planning of a separate educational organization, 3. Use of technical media and 4. Organizing of seminars or meetings between students and teachers for two way communication.

Document

"A record of a work on paper or other material fit for easy physical handling, transport across space and preservation through time (S. R. Ranganathan). The term document includes any bibliographic item or micro and physical embodiment is exclusively of one work or is shared by more than one work. It institutes of subject plus language and plus recording material" (S. R. Ranganathan).

Documentation

"Pinpointed, exhaustive and expeditious service of nascent micro thought to specialist" (S. R. Ranganathan).

According Dr. Ranganathan, documentation lays stress on three aspects viz: 1. Nascent thought far more than an old thought; 2. Micro-document; and 3. Specialist readers far more than on general readers.

Documentation Centre

It selects, acquires, organizes and retrieves specific information and documents on demand by its users. It provides services to its users even in anticipation. *Harrod's Lirarians Glossary* defines documentation centre as a "place where publications are received, processed, summarized, abstracted and indexed; where bulletins relating to such material are prepared for distribution to those interested, when research is undertaken, bibliographies prepared and copies and translations are made".

Document Delivery

"Supply of journal articles and other copies on a personal basis, whether these come from other libraries or direct from publishers. The end-user is usually responsible for any fee such as costs for postage or photocopying" (Wikipedia).

Document Imaging

It is the conversion (digitizing of paper documents in to electronic documents) using a scanner or similar device, and the subsequent storage and management of those electronic images. This would be of immense value to organize and present comprehensive picture for decision support.

Document Literacy

It means the knowledge and skills required to locate and use information embodied in various formats including job applications, payroll forms, transportation schedules, maps, tables and graphics.

Drupal

Drupal is a free and open source Content Management System (CMS) written in PHP and distributed under the GNU General Public License. It is used for many different types of websites ranging from small personal blogs to large corporate and political sites including whitehouse.gov.

Dspace

Dspace has been designed and developed by Massachusetts Institute of Technology (MIT) libraries and Hewlett-Packard (HP). Dspace was designed as an open source application so that institutions could run with relatively few resources. It is to support long-term preservation of the digital material stored in the repository. Dspace supports submission, management and access of digital contents. Space can be installed on Linux, Unix and Windows. It is freely available under BSD license. It is a platform that allows users to capture items in any formation – in text, video, audio and data. It provides a way to manage research materials and publications in a professionally maintained repository to give them greater viability and accessibility over time.

Dublin Core Metadata Initiative (DCMI)

It is an organization dedicated to fostering the wide spread adoption of interoperable metadata standards and promoting the development of specialized metadata vocabularies for describing resources to enable more intelligent resource discovery systems.

It traces its roots to Chicago at the 2nd International World Wide Web Conference, October 1994. The initial brainstorming lead to NCSA and OCLC holding a joint Workshop to discuss Metadata Semantics in Dublin, Ohio, March, 1995.

Dura space's Dura cloud

It provides Open Source Repository Solutions by undertaking turnkey projects for organizations and libraries to enable them to share scholarly literature using Dspace and Feroda Commons. It is dedicated in sustaining and improving Feroda and Dpace two of the most dominant source repository solutions.

E

EBRARY

It was established in 1999 by Christopher Warnock and KelinSayar in Palo Alto, California. It is an online digital library with full text collection of over 70,000 scholarly e-books. The database contains books, journals, magazines, maps and other publications in the field of Business, Economics, Computer, Technology, Engineering, Humanities, Life and Physical Sciences and Social and Behavioral Sciences from over 500 publishers.

ERNET (The Educational and Research Network)

This was initiated and implemented by Department of Electronics (DOE) with UND funding initially, has over 400 organizations connected within India and neighboring countries. These institutions are mainly academic and research organizations, non-government organizations and to limited extent private international organizations. It is supported by several backbone sites covering DOE (New Delhi), IIT (Madras), IISc (Bangalore), IMTECH (Chandigarh), VECC (Calcutta), IUCA (Pune), OVCST (Bombay) and Central University of Hyderabad which enable organizations located at different geographical locations to access various services of Internet.

E-book

1. A computer file / electronic copy of printed book that needs a device such as PC or PDA or Web, to access and read.

   Advantages: Easy to carry, saving space, convenience, saving money and time and ease of use.

2. A published book in the electronic form (e-form). The form includes CD-ROMs, Web based resources and special devices such as personal digital assistants (PDAs) and Cell phones.

3. Any piece of electronic text regardless of size or composition (a digital object) but excluding journal publications made available electronically (or optically) for any device (handheld or deskbound) that includes a screen (Edwards & Lonsdale).

Characteristics : The following are some of the important characteristics of E-Book. 1. Easy portability, 2. Instant access to information, 3.Easy Searchability, 4. Annotation, 5.Linking with multi-media, 6. Material can be preserved for longer period, 7. Includes online dictionary and link to other sites, 8. Publishing and distribution costs lower than print media.

E-Administration

It is government to government interaction. This includes statewide and inter departmental information networks making the whole administration e-administration. It includes e-secretariat, e-laws, e-police, e-judiciary and so on.

E-Book Aggregators

The companies that are not involved in the work of publishing, but they collect e-books from various publishers and make it available to libraries through specific hardware and software platform. Some leading aggregators in e-book market are E-library, Net Library, Safari, Books@Ovid, etc.

E-Book(s)

An E-book or an electronic book is an electronic or digital equivalent of a printed books. E-books is either read on personal computers or on dedicated hardware device known as E-book device or E-book reader. An E-book consists of electronic content originating from traditional books, reference material or magazines that is downloaded from the internet and viewed through any number of hardware devices.

Advantages : 1. Thousands of books may carried together on one device, 2. Approximately 500 E-books can be stored on one CD. 3. Size and font may be adjusted, 4. It can be instantly copied, 5. Distributed at low cost, 6. Distributed instantly, 7. Errors may be easily corrected, 8. Economically and environmentally viable by cutting down on paper usage, 9. Does not wear overtime, 10. No risk of Vandalism, damage etc. on the pages.

Disadvantages : 1. Can be incompatible with new hardware and software, 2. Required care in handling and storage of files, 3. Can restrict printing, 4. Devices are expensive and can be lost, stolen and damaged, 5. Batteries may run out, 6. Average E-book price is too expensive when compared with printed edition, 7. Many readers prefer paper and print to a computer screen, 8. E-books can be easily copied violating copyright laws, 9. Reading can be hard or even harmful to eyes.

E-Bookshops

The buyers can search for their required books on the web portal of the e-bookshops by sitting in their houses or workplaces, order online and received books at their doorsteps. E.g. Amazon, Barnes and Noble, The Book Depository, Blackwell, etc.

E-Brochure

It is a multimedia replace meant for direct mail paper. It consists of a highly interactive programme using still images, graphics, animation, sound, text and data. Motion pictures, video is seldom used to storage and performance limitations. E-brochure play a very positive role in online communication.

E-Business

The services which business houses avail from government and the information and taxes which government procures from such houses come indirect. It is government to business and vice-versa.

E-Cataloguer

The purpose of developing a cataloguer is to create bibliographic database of library documents in a library without keying the data. E-cataloguer helps the library professionals to create large library databases quickly and easily with minimum human intervention.

E-Choupals

This system was introduced by International Business Division of ITC Ltd., in June 2000. The ISO Group is responsible for processing, procuring and exporting agricultural commodities in six States viz: Andhra Pradesh, Karnataka, Madhya Pradesh, Maharashtra, Rajasthan and Uttar Pradesh.

The number of e-Choupals installed is about 4100 covering 21000 villages empowering 24 lakh farmers.

E-Commerce

It is a modern business terminology that addresses the needs of organisations, merchants and consumers to cut costs while improving the quality of goods and services and increasing the speed of service delivery. As far as library is concerned, e-commerce means promoting the library as a profitable entity through online marketing of information products and services and generates revenue in a variety of ways for the library.

Need : 1. To increase revenue, 2. To provide quality service, 3. To market library products, 4. To meet the consumer needs efficiently, and 5. To provide value added service.

E-Content World

In the e-content world, publishers have taken direct and strategic control of content, its IP (Intellectual Property) ownership and its delivery and usage through the entire legal lifecycle of the content until the copyright period expires. Technology will facilitate them to maintain just one copy of the content and a few mirror copies, if need be, to serve the needs of all global users through internet.

E-Democracy

It means citizen to government or government to citizen and interactions made at several occasions like at the time of elections, paying taxes or information for census data. Broadly, e-democracy refers to processes and structures that encompass all forms of electronic communication between government and citizen.

E-Depot System

The Konin Klijeke Bibliotheck (KB) (National Library of the Netherlands) is the first national library in the world to start and own an operational system for the deposit and long term preservation of digital publications. The KB ensures libraries; publishers and end users that the information stored in the archive will outlast the transience of digital documents. In addition, e-Depot offers publishers a durable check on archival formats as well as guidance on how to create the most durable electronic publications. The library has entered into an agreement with 30 + Publishers and libraries to achieve the scholarly content. As of November 2007, the Depot has acquired more than 10 million digital objects most of them are publications by international publishers.

E-Education

It involves e-teaching and e-learning along with the various administrative and strategic measure needed to support teaching and learning in an internet environment. It will incorporate a local regional, national and international view of education.

E-Governance

It is the process of service delivery and information dissemination to citizens through electronic means. **The Objectives** of e-governance is as follows: 1. To improve and faster service delivery to citizens, 2. To increase efficiency in the governmental processes, 3. To create transparency and corruption free in all transitions., 4. To empower citizens through updated information, and 5. To make aware the citizens their rights and duties.

E-Grandhalaya

It is an open source library automation software for public libraries designed and developed by Karnataka State Unit of National Informatics Centre (NIC) Bangalore. Version 1.0 was released in January 2003. NIC Library, New Delhi was also given responsibility to implement E-Grandhalaya in North India. The version 2.0 of the E-Grandhalaya was released during 2005 by NIC headquarters **library** at New Delhi. Version 3.0 was released in 2007. The features of version 3.0 are: 1. LAN / WAN based connectivity is possible to update and create database from Clint PCs, 2. New service based reports are available, 3. Barcode numbers have been omitted, 4. To make the software multilingual, new technology from Microsoft has been used, 5. Indian languages were supported by the Windows Operating System.

E-Granth

It was the first ever initiative by ICAR designed with 'open access' as one of its objectives. The consortium sponsored by NAIP (ICAR) has 12 partner institutions. They will be using *New Gen Lib* or *Koha* software for implementing Online Public Access Catalogue (OPAC). The local catalogues would be converted into union catalogue which would eventually be uploaded to *World Cat 21*. The library resources of three institutions viz: *1. IARI, New Delhi, 2. Indian Veterinary Research Institute, Izatnagar* and *3. University of Agricultural Sciences, Bangalore* will be digitized to searchable Portable Document Format (PDF) documents. The digitized documents would then be hosted on D-space / E-prints based digital repository.

E-Gyankosh

It is a National Digital Repository. In October 2005, Indira Gandhi National Open University (IGNOU) initiated the development of knowledge repository of online learning resources for storing, indexing, preserving, disseminating and sharing digital learning resources developed by the Open and Distance Learning (ODL) institutions in India. At present e-learning is more advanced and dynamic concepts of social networking, personal learning environments and mobile learning classroom teaching by using ICT applications. It is an online learning environment for distance learners.

E-Information

"A broad term that encompasses abstracting and indexing services, electronic journals and their full text materials, the offering of information aggregators, article delivery services, etc, which can be accessed via remote networks from information providers or locally mounted by a consortium or one of its member libraries". (The International Coalition of Library Consortia (ICOLC).

E-Information Literacy

1. It is the ability to properly send and evaluate electronic resources, tools and services and apply it for lifelong learning process.
2. It is the delivery of information, training or education programmes via electronic media that includes wide range of electronic communications like internet, satellite broadcast, interactive television, CD-ROM, DVD, audio and video tapes, etc.

Need : 1. Rapid increase in quantity and variety of formats of recorded information; 2. Hybrid scenario of information and communication technology, 3. Pressing demand for faster delivery of information, 4. Libraries expansion beyond walls, 5. Diffusion and dispersal of information, 6. Interdisciplinary growth of literature, 7. Emergence of data mining and 8. Increased fragility and vulnerability of Information.

Ways of conduction E-Information Literacy Programmes : 1.Classroom lectures, 2. Seminars / Workshops, 3.Trade literature describing guidelines, 4.Audio materials, 5.Individual instructions, 6. Industry-academia interface, 7. Online courses / tutorials, and 8. Conducting refresher courses.

E-Journals

1. A publication whose primary means of delivery to subscribers is through a computer file.

2. "Any serial produced, published and distributed via e-networks such as BITNET and Internet. E-journals may be defined very broadly as any journals, magazines, newsletter, or type of e-serial publication which is available over the Internet" (McMillan).
3. "A journal that is available in electronic form through online host called e-journal" (F. W. Lancaster).

These are one of the most important services rendered by the digital and electronic libraries. E-Journals are published in electronic format and distributed to its users via Internet. E-Journals are also known as 'digital journals' or 'online journals' or 'Electronic serials'. The main feature of e-journal is, its ready accessibility and it does not consume much time for printing and mailing.

Characteristics: 1. Speed of publication and delivery, 2. Available worldwide on Internet, 3. E-publishing can achieve significant savings, 4. Internet supports sound and images with text, 5. Provide facilities of downloading and printing of required article(s), 6. Provide link to related articles, 7. Conservation and preservation problem will be minimum, 8. Cost involved in publishing and distributing of e-journals will be less than print.

Need : 1. To support simultaneously paper and e-methods of knowledge dissemination, 2. Inter disciplinary research and new fields have increased the scientists demand, 3. Academics to distribute their own resources using new technology and 4. To provide remote access, timely access simultaneously to more than one user.

Criteria for selection : 1. Content, 2. Added values, 3. Functionality, 4. Technical consideration, 5. Licensing agreement and 6. Service impact.

Features: 1. Can be delivered on to the desktop, 2. More than one person can read them at a times, 3. Entire text can be searched, 4. Can include multimedia and graphics, in color, at marginal costs, 5. Can be published more quickly than print publications, 6. Can be interactive and foster online exchange of ideas, 7. Can make hyperlinks, 8. Articles can be retrieved directly through links from abstracting and indexing databases and 9. Content can be reproduced, forwarded and modified.

E-Journal Consortium

It is a group of different independent libraries or information centers with the aim of sharing e-journals subscription by individual libraries for joint accomplishment of specific objective. For example publishers like Elsevier, Kluwer, Academic Publishers, Blackwell and others encourage libraries to develop their own consortia to share e-journals, each with its own set of policies and pricing models.

Advantages : 1. Unlimited access to varied journals including back volumes. 2. Advantageous pricing system offering discounts. 3. Availability of additional funding from Government an Non-Governmental Organizations. 4. Simplification of financial transactions. 5. Increased cooperation and coordination among partners of consortia. 6. Development of new technical and other skills of library staff.

Disadvantages : In the absence of centralized administrative control coordination among partners may be difficult. 2. Work among library staff may increase. 3. Difficult to bring coordination of policy among participating institutions and consortia policy. 4. Audit restrictions may cropup for spending money in consortia. 5. Functioning of consortia may hamper due to non-availability of skilled manpower, 6. Inadequate promotion of services may lead to underutilization of resources.

E-Journal Consortia in India

The following are some of the e-journal consortia in India: 1. The National Knowledge Resources Consortium

(NKRC), 2.Indian National Digital Library in Engineering Sciences and Technology (INDEST), 3. UGC-Info net Digital Library Consortium (presently E-Sodh-Sindhu), National Medical Library's Electronic Resources in Medicine Consortium(ERMED), DBT e-Library Consortium(DeLCON) and DRDO E-Journal Consortium.

E-Learning

1. It is defined as instruction delivered on a computer via internet or CD-ROM. It can be self-paced or instructor led and includes media in the form of text, streaming video and audio and builds user knowledge to improve organizational functioning. E-learning commonly refers to training delivered electronically in an organizational setting while online learning is used to differentiate courses delivered via the internet in educational settings.

Role and Importance of E-learning : 1. It is being used to impart distance education, 2. It helps users in making use of e-resources, 3. The Librarians need to aware the internet and the resources available therein, 4. To train both the librarians and also users for the use of e-resources.

2. It is a combination of learning methods and technologies to provide high value based integrated learning, any time, any place. It is a flexible, quick and high quality learning method that uses various learning tools of the internet.

Elements : 1. Content delivery methods, 2. Live broadcasting, 3. Video-on Demand, 4. Interactive Communications.

Characteristics : 1. Freedom of learning anywhere, any time and at any place, 2. Individual privacy in learning, 3. Printed material reduced or totally eliminated, 4. Increased use of information technologies, 5. Provides borderless education, 6. Industrialized education or e-business based approach to education, 7. Provides lifelong education to anybody who is interested, and 8. Enjoyable infotainment based education.

Advantages: 1. Convenient for instructions and learners to access resources 'any time, any place', 2. Course contents are cheaper than printed material, 3. Resources can be recalled several times, 4. Reduces travel time of learners, 5. Allows learners to save to select, retrieve and access their wanted learning material, 6. Stimulates learners to access a variety of digital resources on WWW, 7. It assists learners to become IT and information literate, 8. It offers opportunity to develop digital resourcecenter, 9. Fosters interaction and dialogue among instructors and e-learners, 10. More than one user can access resources simultaneously from different platforms and locations and 11. It is easy to update the resources on the web.

E-Library

"A collection of networked digital information sources and associated technical and managerial infrastructure" (Stephen Pinfield). The terms 'Electronic library', 'E-Library', 'Online Library' and 'digital library' or 'Virtual Library' are used synonymously.

E-Resources : E-books, e-text archives, Online text collections, E-Journals / Online Journals, Databases, Websites, CD-ROM Databases, DVDs, Microfilms, Microfiche, Audio Cassettes and Video Cassettes.

It facilitates easy and quick searching, E-books downloading, inter-library loaning, copying, sending and getting feedback etc.

Advantages : 1. Unequivocal and equivalent accessibility to all, 2. Round the clock accessibility around the world, 3. Unlimited storage capacity, 4. Provides unlimited source material by inter-library lending, 5. Speed and quick exploration, 6. E-Books downloading facility, 7. Faster and greater feedback through internet, 8. Cheaper and affordable to both Individual and Institution, 9. More flexible.

Disadvantages : 1. Limited accessibility, 2. Lack of sufficient technical knowledge and known-how, 3. Difficulty in reaching on computer screen, 4. Excessive information and credibility.

E-Mail (Electronic Mail)

It is a generic name for non-interactive communication of text, data, image and / or voice message between a sender and recipient/s by utilizing telecommunication links.

Characteristics: 1. Overseas communications and high traffic communications are cheap, 2. Increases speed of information transfer, 3. It is reliable and accurate, 4. Messages can be sent to multiple recipients simultaneously, 5. Transfer of images and other types of documents across the Internet is possible, 6. It is not necessarily private.

E-PG Pathasala

The Ministry of Human Resource Development (MHRD), Govt. of India has started project, National Mission on Education through Information and Communication Technology (NME-ICT) to initiate and accelerate the ICT-enabled Higher Education. NME-ICT has sanctioned to produce e-content in 77 subjects for PG level. It was proposed to create and maintain the e-contents with high quality based on curriculum and syllabus interactivity in various subjects in all disciplines like natural and mathematical sciences, social sciences, arts and humanities and linguistics and languages. The developed e-contents are available in open access and also accessible through Sakshat Portal.

E-Print Archives

An E-print is a reprint in electronic or web-based format. E-prints are archived in repository format which is generally being developed to house the research publications of researchers in a particular institute. The aim of such E-Print repositories is to make research freely available. A simple and practicable solution is open access through e-print archive. A researcher can self-archive his articles on his website and enhance its accessibility.

E-Prints

E-Prints was developed at the University of Southampton, U.K. with the first version of the software publicly released in 2000. As the first professional software platform for building high quality OAI-Compliant repositories, E-prints is already established as the earliest and fastest way to setup repositories of open access research literature, scientific data, theses, reports and multimedia. E-prints 3 is a major leap forward in functionality, giving even more control and flexibility to repository managers, depositors, researchers and technical administrators. The latest version of E-Prints: v 3.3 is available for Debinan / Ubuntu, Red hat / Fedora and Windows.

Features : 1. It is an open-source software distributed under GPL Licensing, 2. It has multilingual support and available on Linux Platform, 3. Metadata is stored in DBMS and on request displayed in XML format, 4. One digital object can have more than one file, 5. Authentic users can be created with rested responsibility, 6. Work-flow can be established and online editors can edit metadata, 7. Online submission is supported in other words it supports self-archiving, 8. Repository displays the recent additions, 9. Software supports simple search by name of author, title and soon, 10. Collection can be created of pre-prints, post-prints and audio-visual streams and so on.

E-Publishing (EP)

1. It is the publishing process where the manuscripts are submitted in electronic format, edited, printed and even distributed to readers by employing computers and telecommunication. Thus the fusion of electronics, computer and communication technologies together for publishing can be termed as EP to denote any information source published in electronic form.

2. An integrated production of documents using digitally stored documents, computerized composition and electronic printing systems.
3. The use of electronic media, computers and telecommunications to deliver information to users in electronic form or from electronic sources (Hawkins et al).

Advantages : 1. Fast and easy access to information, 2. Facilitates better quality of service, 3. Data can be maintained up-to-date, 4. Ensures timely publication which is of utmost importance to research community, 5. Allows dual publishing i.e. publishing of articles relevant to two different subjects in more than one journal, 6. It is cost-effective compared to conventional form of publishing, 7. It is environmental friendly as it does not require hundreds and thousands trees for paper making.

Categories of E-Publishing: 1. E-books, E-journals, 3. E-zine (magazines), 4. E-theses and dissertations, 5. E-reference tools.

E-Republic

"The concept e-republic is derived from elements of self determination, cosmopolitanism, technological idealism and civil society" (Pankaj Sharma). The people who share similar values, interests or heritage are free to form an affiliation across geographical boundaries and are entitled to establish a governance structure. It means interaction between Netizens at global level.

E-Resource(s)

1. An electronic product that delivers a collection of data, it may be text referring to full text databases, electronic journals, image collection, other multimedia collections. These may be delivered on tape, via Internet and so on can be easily managed.

2. A comprehensive term for all types of media for recording, communicating and preserving knowledge. These include: books, journals, newspapers, maps, microforms, manuscripts in electronic forms. It is any portable medium of recorded information which can be preserved through time.

Types : E-Journal, E-books, E-Groups, E-Lists, Library Networks, Databases, Library Websites, Web OPACS Digital Archives, Bulletin Boards, Web-exhibitions, Virtual Conferences, Virtual help Dsks.

Characteristics : 1. Encompassing everything, 2. Organized arbitrarily, 3. Occupying no physical space, 4. Full content searchable, 5. Elimination of space, time and cost constraints, 6. Public domain of information, 7. Easy usability, 8. Affordability and 9. Accessibility.

Types : E-books, E-Journals, Online Databases, Websites, Electronic Theses and Dissertation (ETD), OPAC's.

Advantages : Multi access, speed, functionality, content ease of access and retrieval, up-to-date, Durability, Low Cost of Production, Supports search capabilities, can be updated more easily and reduce storage space, can be easily managed.

Disadvantages : Initial high infrastructure and installation cost, Hardware and software compatibility issues between publishers and users, causes more concern about copyright issues, requirement of efficient manpower.

E-Society

It deals with comprehensive relationship between public agencies and other institutions like private sector, service providers, non-profit and community organizations or non-government organizations. "The rationale is to create a strong economic, social and political fabric within the society by using the potential of ICTs to strengthen current information connections and to build new information connections between institutions" (P.D. Kaushik).

E-ShodhSindhu

UGC-INFONET has started the consortium of e-journals subscription for select University Libraries. Now more than 217 University Libraries in India have been connected through this consortium and it is being planned to provide this service through higher bandwidth of internet connection which will be given to the rest of the University Libraries in a phased manner. At present it is known as a ShodhSindhu. It provides latest as well as archival access to more than 15000 core subjects and peer-reviewed journals and millions of bibliographic, citation and factual databases various subjects from a large number of publishers and journal aggregators.

E-Teachers

These are the new generation of teachers who will work in an internet environment in both regular and virtual class room situations. They will build new concepts of working in time and space. E-teachers collaborate, build and discover new learning communities and explore resources as they interact with information, materials and ideas with their students and colleagues.

Educational Data Mining (EDM)

It is an evolving research area concerned with unique data emerging from educational environment and by applying various approaches for understanding students in better way. EDM discovers data patterns by focusing on development of new algorithms and tools. EDM develops approaches to analyze the data collected while learning and teaching process by applying techniques from machine learning, statistics and data mining.

Educational Media

It refers to all kinds of teaching and technical aids provided for education and instruction which is being increasingly applied for better results.

Electronic Book

1. It is popularly referred to as e-book, digital book or e-edition printed book. It is a book-length publication in digital form consisting text, images or both that are readable on computers or other electronic devices.
2. "The result of integrating classical book structure, or rather the familiar concept of a book, with features that can be provided within an electronic environment is referred to as an electronic book (e-book), which is intended as an interactive on a computer". (International Encyclopedia of Information and Library Science, 2ndEdn, 2003).

Some of the important benefits : 1. One access point to thousands of monographs, 2. Any time anywhere access, 3. Automatic Check-in, 4. Less space required, 5. Trusted content known for is quality, 6. It will be accessible quickly for acquisition, 7. Reader can change font size to suit their personal preference, 8. Cost less than conventional printed books, 9. Easy to search a particular topic in the book, and 10. Provides multi-media information, full text searching, citation formatting and portability.

Electronic Data Interchange (EDI)

It is a "computer to computer transfer of commercial or administrative transactions using an agreed standard to structure the data pertaining to that transaction" (U.N. definition). It is focussed on transfer of electronic information normally provided in digital documents. The benefits of using EDI over tradition mechanisms include cost saving, speed, error minimization and security.

Electronic Document Delivery Service (EDDS)

It is referred to as one part of a multi-stage process. It provides the flexibility to access the required material across the world from a number of sources. It delivers on loan or supplies documents as physical objects. It provides access to information not held or immediately available in the library and information centre approached for the purpose.

Basic Components : 1 A document store or archive having sending station with a data communication interface, 2. A means of links with PSTN, PSDN, ISD Net, 3. A receiving station having PC with suitable interface.

Advantages : 1. It is the quick way of getting the required document/s over webserver / Internet / E-mail, 2. It can be stored / copied / multiple copies can be made, 3. It is easy to handle / carry on floppy / to take printouts, 4. It is possible to edit / add / delete anything and can be sent.

Disadvantages : Some of them are: 1. While scanning, there may errors on the scanned document, 2. Non-availability of similar software at the receiving end, 3. Power disruption may cause a delay in getting the required document, 4. Compression techniques are needed at both the ends, and 5. Some users may feel that they read hard copy only.

Electronic Information Resources (EIRs)

Those library resources that can only be accessed via the use of computing devices such as computers, tablets and smartphones.

Electronic Ink

It is a developing technology that could have a huge impact on the media and publishing industries. It could be used to create a newspaper or book that updates itself. The technology could also be used on billboards, clothing, walls and homes to allow content to appear.

Electronic Newspaper

It is self-contained, reusable and refreshable version of a traditional newspaper that acquired and holds all information in the newspaper electronically.

Electronic Library

1. The resources of an electronic library are in electronic form and functions are fully automatic. Sometimes resources are online. Offline resources are computer disc, CD-ROM, DVD-ROM, e-book, -journal, audio CD, etc. conventional circulation system for the off-line resources exists. Digitization of electronic library material is its optimal activity.

2. An electronic library is "(1) a service, (2) an architecture, (3) a set of information resources, databases of text, numbers, graphics, sound, video, etc. (4) a set of books and capabilities to locate, retrieve and utilize the information resources available" (Bogmann, 1999).

Electronic Publishing (EP)

EP is a process for production of typeset-quality documents containing text, graphics, pictures, tables, equations, etc. In general it is used to mean any information source published in electronic form. EP is a combination of Electronic, Computer and Communication technologies which contributed for its emergence. It includes sources like magnetic tapes, video discs and databases.

Advantages: 1. It allows documents to be interactive, 2. Very easy to access and save the time of the user, 3. Documents published on-line are readily available on WWW, 4. Reissuing of a complete document is relatively fast and less expensive, 5. No loss of quality over time for the information in digital format, 6. Data in digital form can be quickly and perfectly duplicated in to a new media, 7. It is eco-friendly, 8. Electronic formats are more economical than printed formats, 8. Allows for instant correction and updating of information at any time, 9. Can be accessed from anywhere and it any time, 10. Can incorporate what is left and archival purpose, 11. Disk based distribution is a better option for storage, and 12. E-version journals are available in advance of printed versions.

Electronic reference

It is interpersonal reference information management using electronic means for the Patron query and for reference response. Libraries have employed this model using telephones earlier. E-mail has added new dimension to the reference relationship. Tools such as E-mail, subject gateways, FAQs and electronic libraries and interactive tools like chat-rooms, virtual reference desk, etc. are replacing the conventional means of reference enquiries.

Electronic resource/s

1. An "electronic resource or e-resource is defined as any work encoded and made available for access through the use of a computer. It includes electronic data available by remote access and direct access (fixed media). Remote access (e-resources) refers to the use of e-resources via computer networks. Direct access refers to the use of electronic resources via carriers, e.g.: discs, cassettes, cartridges designed to be inserted in to computer device or is auxiliary equipment.

2. Any cohesive publication in digital form that is being marketed or any electronic product that delivers a collection of data, be it text, numerical, graphical or time based, as a commercially available resource and includes full-text databases, electronic journals, image collections, multimedia products, collection of numerical data" (S. D. Lee and F. Boyle).

Characteristics : 1. Potentially enormous, 2. Not organized and comprehensive of everything, 3. Physical space is not required, 4. Search operations are wide in range, 5. Full content search is feasible, 6. Constraints which are common in conventional libraries are not in e-resources.

Advantages: 1. Low cost of production, 2. Saves time by providing easy access, 3. Easy duplication, 4. Integration of different media, 5. Saves library storage space, 6. Allows remote access, 7. Enables simultaneous access, 8. Facilitates access to physically challenged persons, 9. Eco-friendly, 10. Provides CAS to all user community.

Disadvantages : 1. Required high cost for technology infrastructure, 2. Lack of compatibility among different publishers, 3. Problems in hardware and software compatibility, 4.Copyright violation problem, 5.Lack of awareness on I. T. Skills for use of e-resources, 6. Libraries face a number of problems relating new media, 7. Subscription to material in e-media are more expensive than traditional print form.

Electronic Resource Management

It refers to procedure adopted by modern libraries for selection, licensing, implementation and maintenance and review.

Electronic Thesis and Dissertation (ETD)

"A ETD is a document that explains the research or scholarship of a researcher / student. It is expressed in a form simultaneously suitable for machine archives and worldwide retrieval. The ETD is similar to its paper predecessor. It has figures, tables, foot-notes and references. It has a title page with author's name, the official name of the University, the degree sought and the names of Committee Members.

Electronic Works

These include: Computer Programme, databases, related documentation (both in Print and electronic form) to be used as manuals by program users. It also includes works like programming languages needed for system development, computer networks, including the Internet and the resources available on the net.

E-mail Publishing

It is popular choice among readers who enjoy the ease of

receiving news items, articles and short newsletters in their e-mail post. The ease of delivery and production of e-mail newsletters has led to the development of a massive number of available e-mail newsletters, mailing lists and discussion lists on a large variety of topics.

Embedded Librarian

Librarians out of libraries and creates a new model of library and information work. It emphasizes the importance of forming a strong working relationship between the librarian and a group or team of people who need librarian's information expertise" (David Shumaker).

Constituents

1. Developing relationship with user.
2. Understanding and catering to their information needs.
3. Sharing their needs.
4. Providing adequate information for achievements of those needs.
5. Customized, active and high value contribution towards achievement of their needs.
6. Becoming an integral part of information seeker.

Characteristics

1. It is a process which builds relationships so that they can gain deeper insights into what users are doing and how they would utilize information provided by the library.
2. Embedded Librarians are anticipatory and suggest ways of accomplishing tasks that others on the team would not think of ways that save the team's time and effort.
3. Embedded librarian works in groups and collaborate with other members so as to achieve team's efforts instead of individual interest.
4. Embedded librarians are technocratic and build strong relationships and provide the value based services to the

user concerned.

5. Embedded librarianship builds partnership and is more focused on achieving the desired ends mutually.

Embedded Librarianship

"It is distinctive innovation that moves the librarians out of libraries and creates a new model of library and information work. It emphasizes the importance of forming a strong working relationship between the librarian and a group or team of people who need the librarian's information expertise" (Shumaker).

Emotional Intelligence

It is a form of social intelligence that involves the ability to monitor one's own and others' feelings and emotions to discriminate among them, and to use this information to guide one's thinking and action.

Encyclopaedic Centres

A Centre which provides comprehensive information services in which all the essential information on a given subject is collected and repackaged. For example '*The Wealth of India*'. It belongs to a special division of the publications Directorate of CSIR (India) located in the then INSDOC Building, New Delhi. Through the publication of *The Wealth of India* and associated compilations and information services, this Unit attempts to provide current information about India useful to national economic, technical and scientific development efforts.

Functions : 1. Acquire and store all material of interest in respect of geographic, ethnic or subject, 2. Serves as a permanent depository of such material, 3. Provides bibliographic services related to this collection, 4. Publishers bibliographical information about the collection, 5. Administer a decentralized depository system for the collection to facilitate greater access.

Energy (Action) [E]

The fundamental category represents concepts that represent action, treatment, evaluation, diagnosis, calculation, control, examination, impact, disease, foreign relations, morphology, grammar, etc. Example: Disease. In the Main Class (MC) Medicine 'Disease' comes under Energy Facet.

Entity

1. "An existent, concrete or conceptual, which is thing or idea" (S. R. Ranganathan).
2. It is defined "as anything (physical or abstract) in the real world about which one wants to keep data, facts or store descriptive information in a database record. An entity may be tangible object with physical existence such as, a particular person, an employee, a library member, a book, a serial, a chair or a table. It may be nontangible object with conceptual existence or an abstract concept such as an event, transaction, a job, a procedure, a subject of study or a university" (M. M. Kashyap).

Entry

An entry is a unit record that contains information (or data) about a bibliographic item on a card or displayed on a computer screen. A bibliographic record displayed on a screen, in a card catalogue or documentation list provides general or specific information about a bibliographic item or items.

Environmental Information System, India (ENVIS)

ENVIS was established by the Ministry of Environment and Forests, Government of India in 1982 to provide information to decision makers, policy makers, planners, scientists, etc., all over the country. It is a decentralized network information system consisting of a Focal Point in the Ministry for coordinating the activities of a chain of 24 subject centres known as ENVIS Centres located in various prestigious institutions / organizations spread all over the country.

Objectives

Long-term Objectives : 1. To buildup repository and dissemination centre in Environmental Science and Engineering, 2. To buildup modern technologies of information, acquisition, processing, storage, retrieval and dissemination of information and 3.To support and promote research, development and innovation in environment information technology.

Short-term Objectives : 1. To provide national environmental information service relevant to present needs, 2. To buildup storage, retrieval and dissemination capabilities, 3. To promote national and international cooperation and liaison for exchange of environmental related information, 4. To promote, support and assist education and training programmes and 5. To promote exchange of information among developing countries. (Harjit Singh).

Ergonomics

1. The science of designing the job to fit the worker and not forcing the worker to fit the job.
2. "Ergonomics is the study of the relationship between the workers and the working environment and the equipment they use" (E Collins Dictionary).
3. It is the study of people's efficiency in their working environment.

Expert systems

These are "Computer Programmes composed of knowledge base that contains the information supplied by the expert and an inference engine that applied the appropriate information from knowledge base to a specific problem" (T.N. Holthoff).

Characteristics : 1. Limited to "a specific domain of expertise, 2. Able to reason with uncertain data, 3. Able to explain itself in a sensible way, 4. Delivering advice as output,

5. Designed to grow incrementally, 6. Typically rule based, 7. Always restricted to a narrow domain of expertise.

Advantages: 1. Provide new mechanisms for capturing information in a very quick and verifiable form in respect of collection of knowledge elements, 2. Knowledge can easily be updated and extended, 3. Users may be able to learn more from accumulated knowledge and 4. User gains confidence because of explanation facility of the system.

Ex-Libriscloud

It is leading library software vendor from USA who initially developed most of the current products as locally implemented solutions and at a later stage, adapted them to a hosted environment. The company's next generation library system, Alma, was conceived as a cloud based service to transform the traditional management of library resources. It besides ensuring considerable savings in total cost, involved in the implementation of software and the use of centralized cloud service enables libraries to easily influence the collaborative efforts of the library community to provide effective services for the users (SaritKozokin).

F

FSTA (Food Science & Technology Abstracts)

It is an internationally recognized world's leading Food Science & Technology Abstracts database from the International Food Information Service (IFIS), Shionfield, Reading, U.K. It comprehensively covers every aspect of food science, food technology and food related human nutrition for all commodities including basic food science, bio-technology, toxicology, Packaging and engineering, etc. It has over 600,000 records with 2000 records added each month. Over 1,800 journals including reviews, standards, legislations, patents, books, theses and conference proceedings plus other regular publications in over 40 languages are being scanned for relevant material for FSTA.

Facebook

It is a social networking service and website launched in February 2004, owned by and founded by Mark Zuakerberg and his friends. M. R. Devilters described Facebook as "One of the most favorite Social Networking site (SNS) where one meets his / her friend's write 'walls' of each other's and renew friendship. It is a site where one can able to see his / her friend's latest pictures and activities".

Features : 1. Allows people to keep in touch with their near and dear, 2. Freely accessible to all, 3. Increase the opportunity of better learning and easy knowledge sharing, 4. Users can access and disseminate updated information easily, 5. It is more successful and socially impactful, 6. It has good privacy setting and given very well security.

Facetometrics

The quantitative methods involved in the selection of keywords from the research articles followed by frequency analysis and the frequency analysis marks key word clusters indicating active research topics of the subject. The name given to this type of study is *Facetometrics*.

Facsimile

It is a copy or reproduction of an old book, manuscript, map, art or item of historical value and importance that is as true to the original source as possible. It differs from other forms of reproduction by attempting to replicate the source as accurately as possible in terms of scale, color, condition and other material qualities.

Federated search

It is an information retrieval technology that allows

simultaneous search of multiple searchable resources. In this process a user makes a single query request which is distributed to the search engines participating in the federation. The federated search then aggregates the results that are received from search engines for presentation to the user. It is also known as: Meta search, broadcast search, cross searching, parallel search and a variety of other names.

Benefits: 1. Enhanced information discovery, 2. Ability to search multiple repositories without having to learn the specific search options, 3. Ability to create one portal for all library content, 4. Searching library and non-library content simultaneously.

Advantages: 1. Reduced time it takes to do basic search, 2. Unified access to diverse content sources, 3. Simultaneous searching access all sources, 4. Ability to simple search as well as advanced search, 5. Integrated results which are easy to view and use, 6. Direct links to the native source for further searching and 7. Ability to filter, sort, save, print, export and e-mail search results.

Drawbacks: 1. Lack of uniform authentication standard means, 2. Metadata standards vary by resource, 3. Relevancy ranking in limited by the quality of metadata, 4. Managed as a service, which takes a great deal of resources, 5. Federated search engines cannot improve on the native interface in terms of search accuracy precision and 6. It cannot cover all online library resources.

Federated Search Engines (FSE)

These are a set of processes which have been working in the back-end and provide results in the frontend. When user searches for a topic it searches from different heterogeneous data sources and combine in a systematic way before showing it on the users screen. After combining the searched results it arranges into relevant rank. If a same search result / source comes from different databases, it avoids duplicate entries at the time of display.

Fedora

It is a general purpose digital repository system developed by the Cornell University Information Science and the University of Virginia Library.

Features: 1. It is an open source web services based frame work for managing and delivering digital content, 2. It provides different views for the same document, 3. It can be used as a component in the creation of applications such as institutional repositories and course management systems, 4. It is written in Java and runs as a web application in Tomcat, 5. It supports batch ingest and batch export, 6. User authentication is restricted to administrator and anonymous users.

Five Fundamental Categories (FFC): Postulate

"There are five and only five fundamental categories of isolate, concepts or ideas namely Personality, (Entity), Matter (Attribute or property), Energy (Action), Space and Time" (S. R. Ranganathan).

Format

The structure of records, principally the machine readable ones. A format defines each data element contained in a given type of record, its sequence in the record and physical characteristics.

Formats blog

It is weblog which specializes in specific form of presentation. For example web comics (image blog), or video blog or moblogs (mobile blog) belong to this category.

Free Classification

"It is a kind of analytico-synthetic classification, in which the isolates concurring to determine the subject are simply listed one after another, without any more specification of the relations holding between them (that is, are connected by an unspecific phase relationship" (Jean-Claude Gardin).

Friend blog

It is a distributed networked journal on the web composed of short, frequently updated posts written by friends connected through their similar interests. By connecting the use friend blog all posts would appears in his friends and acquaintances 'Friend Blogs".

Fundamental Requirement for Bibliographic Records

It is essentially a conceptual model and not a data model. It is basically "a framework that identified and clearly defines the entities of interest to users of bibliographic records, the attributes of each entity and the types of relationships that operate between entities" (IFLA).

Fyzee Committee

The then Government of Bombay appointed in 1939 a Committee under the chairmanship of A. A. A. Fyzee to study the existing library conditions in the then Bombay Province and recommend suitable measures for developing and strengthening of public library services. The Committee recommended a phased programme of developing libraries in six stages. The first stage was setting up of a Central Library at Bombay and 3. Regional Libraries. As a result Regional Libraries at Ahmedabad, Dharwad and Poona came into being charged with the responsibility of acting as Regional Deposit Centres for copyright collection in the respective regional languages.

G

G2C (Government to Citizen) Information Service

The Information Technology Departments of the States are responsible for implementing the National e-Governance Plan (NeGP) of he Government of India. Its objective is to take the administration to the doorsteps of the people in order to ensure the Government Services are efficient, transparent and reliable while at the same time ensuring that the life of citizens is made easier. Three major backbone infrastructure requirements for delivery of G2C information services under the e-Governance Projects are: 1. Statewide Area Network, 2. National Data Bank / State Data Centres (SDC), and 3. Common Service Centres (CSC).

GISTNIC (General Information Terminal – National Informatics Centre)

It was designed with an objective to make available general information to public about India, important national and international information, infrastructural and recreational facilities and other static and near static information through a query system.

Objectives : 1. To offer online general information database services to common public by deriving useful information from various existing databases and other information centres, 2. To act as NICNET based communication channel for the Government to assist in disseminating important development information to common people, 3. To popularize informatics culture into lifestyle of common public for improving quality of life.

Online services offered: 1. Statistical profile of India, 2. District level economic indicators, 3. District profiles, 4. University Education Guide of India, 5. Tourist Guide of India, 6. All India Railway Time-table, 7. Hotel Guide of India, 8.

General Information Guide, 9. All India Hospital Directory, 10. Country profiles, 11. World Economy Tables, 12. Industrial Directory of India, 13. Employment Guide, and 14. Investment Guide.

GNU EPrints

It is generic archive software developed by the University of Southampton. It is intended to create a highly configurable web-base archive. GNUEPrints primary goal is to be set up as an open archive for research papers, and the default configuration reflects this, but it could be easily of use for other things such as images, research data, audio archives – anything that can be stored digitally, but one has to make more changes to the configuration.

Features : 1. Standard installation via "configure", 2. Very configurable and adaptable, 3. Can store documents in any format, 4. GNUEPrints can be placed in a configurable, extendible subject hierarchy, 5. Users can subscribe either as authors or readers via web form or automatically processed e-mail account, 6. Authors can have associated media.

Gateway

1. It is a network node in which different e-resources from numerous databases can be searched through a single window on the computer. It is a service to deliver resources to the end user through a single search interface. Its general purpose is to allow the user to find cross-references information from different sources by searching and browsing.

2. A gateway is a network points that acts as an entrance to another network. On Internet, a mode or stopping point can be either a gateway node or a host node. Both the computers of the Internet users and the computers that serve pages to users are host nodes.

Gender digital divide

It leads towards study of digital divide among women. Historically little access to media, communication technologies and the opportunity to build communities and share experience with other on a global basis, lead to the emergence gender digital divide. It is an extension of the digital divide concept and focuses specifically on the inequality of women's access to and use of information technologies.

Geographical Indications

Every region in a country has its claim to fame. For example: China silk, Dhaka muslin, Venetian glass. Each reputation was carefully built up and painstakingly maintained through centuries by the masters of that region. Gradually specific link between the goods and place of production evolved resulting in growth of geographical Indications. Indian Geographical Indications: Darjeeling Tea, Pochampally Ikat, Mysore silk, Solapur Chaddar, Bidriware, etc.

Globalization

It represents the international system that is shaping most societies today. It is a process that is supercharging the interaction and integration of cultures, politics, business and intellectual elements around world. Driven by technology, information and finance, a full spectrum of views exist, some praising, some disparaging as to value of globalization.

Global Patent Index (GPI)

It is an advanced online tool for searching the European Patent Office (EPO) World Wide bibliographic data collection catering more than 80 million patents from EPO's World Wide Patent Data Collection (Over 90 percent granting authorities).

Good Offices Committee (GOC)

It is voluntary organization formed to establish uniform

terms of book supplies to libraries and to ensure a fair working margin to book sellers and an efficient to libraries. The Committee meets at regular intervals and after taking into consideration the fluctuations in currency rates decides on the rates of conversion governing sale of books and periodicals. These rates are widely circulated among the libraries all over India either directly or through book sellers.

Google

The most popular search engine, Google, runs on distributed network of thousands of computers and can therefore carryout fast parallel processing. Parallel processing is a method of computation in which many calculations can be performed simultaneously significantly speeding up data processing. "It has three distinct parts:1. googlebot, a Web Crawler that finds and fetches webpages, 2. The Indexer that sorts every word on every page and stores the resulting index of words in a hue database, 3. The query processor, which compares the search query it received to the index and recommends the documents that it considers most relevant" (S. R. Hatua).

Google Apps

Google Apps cloud services, a multi-tenant, internet scale infrastructure offers faster access to innovation, superior reliability and security and maximum economics of scale as compared to on-premises, hosted and software plus services technologies. It is available free for individuals and organizations, educational institutions and US non-profitable organizations and for price to businesses and organizations.

Google Books

In December 2004 Google announced the beginning of "Google Print" Library Project, made possible by partnership with Harvard University, University of Michigan, the New York Public Library, Oxford and Stanford. The combined collections of these libraries were estimated to exceed 15 million volumes. Subsequently many more libraries joined the project and currently host huge number of digitized books in all subjects, some of which are freely readable.

Google Custom Search

It is an online platform provided by Google that allows web developers to feature specialized information in web searches, refine and categories quarries and create customized search engines based on Google Web Search. Google launched this service on 10.05.2006 (Wikipedia).

Government Documents

1. "Any publication originating in or issued with the imprint of, or at the expense and by the authority of any office of a legally organized government or international organization" *(ALA Glossary of Library and Information Science).*
2. "Publication issued at government expenses or published by authority of a government body" *(Harrod's Librarians Glossary).*

Levels of government documents : a) Central government documents, b) State government documents, c) Local government documents, d) Documents issued by foreign countries and e) International / Inter governmental organizations documents.

Types of Government documents : 1. Administrative Reports, 2. Statistical Reports, 3. Commission and Committee Reports, 4. Research Reports, 5. Bills, Acts, Laws, Codes, etc. 6. Law Reports, digests, etc., 7. Records of proceedings, 8. Rules and Regulations, 9. Periodicals, 10. Maps and Charts, 11. Lists and Bibliographies, 12. Popular Descriptions and 13. Publicity Literature (Mohinder Singh's Classification).

Granthalaya

It is a complete library automation package designed and developed in FoxPro by the INSDOC, New Delhi. This package is available in MS-DOS. *Salient Features:* 1. Modularity, 2. Object Oriented Design, 3. CCF Compatibility, 4. Dictionary concept, 5. Ease of use.

Green Library

"A Library designed to minimize negative impact on the natural environment and maximize indoor environment quality by means of careful site selection, use of natural construction materials and biodegradable products, conservation resources (Water, Energy, Paper, Waste disposal, Recycling, etc.)". (The Online Dictionary of Library and Information Science).

Greenstone

Greenstone is a software for building and distributing digital library collections. It provides a new way of organizing information and publishing it on the internet. It is produced by the New Zeeland Digital Library Project at the University of Waikato and developed and distributed in cooperation with UNESCO and the Human Info NGO. It is open source, multilingual software issued under the terms of the GNU General Public License. The aim is to empower users, particularly in Universities, libraries and other public service institutions to build their own digital libraries. It was originally released in 2000 and programmed in C++ and Pearl and runs on all versions of Windows, Unix / Linux and Mac OS-X.

Features : 1. It is an Open Source Software, 2. It has multilingual support and it is platform independent, 3. It requires Perl, Web Service GDBM, MG (Indexing) and C++, 4. It support Z39.50 and 5. Metadata is stored in SML format and displayed using XSLT on browser, 6. The software supports full-text searching and metadata searching, 7. Individual collections can be developed, 8. It does not support cross-collection searching, 9. Collections cannot be further subdivided and 10. It does have authentication for system administrator.

Greenstone Digital Library Software

It is produced by New Zealand Digital Library Project at the University of Waikato and developed and distributed in cooperation with UNESCO and the Human Info NGO. It is open-source, multilingual software issued under the terms of GNU General Public License. It is under Unix, windows and Mac (OS/X) and General users can downloaded the software from *http://www.greenstone.org/*. It is fully documented in English, French, Spanish and Russian.

Features: 1. It is intended to help people design and build collections quickly and easily. 2. The facilities that a collection provides and the user interface for searching and browsing are highly customizable at many different levels, 3. It is multilingual: currently there are interfaces in Arabic, Chinese, French, Dutch, German, Hebrew, English, Italian, etc., 4. Installing Greenstone building collections require no more than ordinary computer literacy skills.

Grey Literature

1. Information produced at all levels of Government, Academies, Business and Industry in electronic and print formats not controlled by Commercial Publishing i.e. where publishing is not the primary activity of the producing body.
2. "This literature is non-conventional in its production, processing, authorship, format of presentation and has relatively poor bibliographic control. It is that literature which is produced at all levels – governments, business, industry, academics – both in print and electronic formats – but which is not controlled by commercial

publishers" (Pratibha A. Gokhale).

Importance: 1. Improve the quality of output research for quick decision making and avoid duplication, 2. Draft status reports, research reports, surveys, market analysis, unpublished laboratory results, experimental data etc. help researchers, scientists, policy makers, academicians to pursue their field of activity, 3. Development plans, Consultancy reports, documents of civil entitlements, theses, pamphlets, working papers are the basic documents needed for furtherresearch and development about local, regional and national matters.

H

Hard Skills

The skills one gains through formal education, training programs, certifications and on the job training which are domain specific and related strictly to a particular work.

Hardware

It comprises memory (stores of data / information / programs), the Central Processing Unit (CPU) that carries out instructions, the input devices like keyboard / mouse and the output devices like monitor (video display) and printer which presents the information to user. *Architecture of Hardware:* 1. Input, 2. Memory, 3. Brain, 4. Output, 5. Coordinating Unit.

Harvesters

A Harvester works as a service provider to collect metadata from a variety of repositories. It processes the OAI-PMH requests in the scheduled manner. Harvesters include resources, item and record to the repositories. One of the popular harvesting open access software is Public Knowledge

Project (PKP). It is an open source released under GNU General Public License.

Health Information Literacy

1. American Library Association (ALA) defined it as "a set of abilities needed to recognize a health information need and identify information sources, assess the quality of the information and its applicability to a specific situation (Analyze, understand and use), the information to make good health decisions".

2. "The ability to access, understand, apprise and communicate information to engage it the demands of health contexts to provide health across the life course" (Rootmen et.al).

Human Computer Interaction (HCI)

HCI is defined as 'a discipline concerned with design, evaluation and implementation of computing systems for human use and with the study of major phenomena surrounding them". (B. Hewett et.al)

Human Relations

"The social relations between human beings and / or a study of human problems arising from organizational and impersonal relations, especially with reference to employer-employee relationship and the interaction between personal traits, group membership and productive efficiency" (Webster's Third International Dictionary).

Human Resource Development (HRD)

It is a process of increasing knowledge, skills, capabilities and all positive work attitude and values of people working at all levels in public and / or private organizations.

1. L. Nadler defined HRD "as a series of organized activities, conducted with a specified time and designated to produce behavioral changes".

2. "It is process of measurement and reporting of the and value of people as organizational resources. It involves accounting for investment in people and their replacement cost, in addition to accounting for economic value to an organization" (R. Jayagopal).

3. "I is a set of structured and integrated social programmes whose scope and thrust are so defined as to put it into one of the following relations with other developmental strategies (a) as a adjunct, (b) as a complementary or (c) as an alternative strategy.

Hybrid Library (H.L.)

It was designed to bring a range of technologies from different sources together in the context of a working library to explore integrated systems and services in electronic and printed environments. It reflects the transitional state of the Library which today can neither be fully print nor fully digital.

Hyper CD-ROM

This is a "tridimensional multilayer optical memory base on the phenomenon of controlled extinction of the fluorescence. It allows the recording of information inside the "shelves" of a glass disk using laser beams. Such a glass disk has a storing capacity of over 10,000 Giga Bytes (GB) of memory an amazing size in comparison with those developed by the highest level computer terms and benchmarks that allows storing of approximately 10 million books of standard format".

Hypertext / Hypermedia

It is a system which does not simply accumulate fragmentary information, but constructs an associative network by connecting related information and enables associative retrieval. When a multimedia programme is developed in a hyper-text environment, the resulting product is called hypermedia. All the hyper media products are multimedia products, but not vice-versa. The basic difference between hypermedia and multimedia is in the organization and linkages of information fragments. The information fragments in multimedia are organized linearly but in hypermedia these are organized non-linearly with links to each other.

I

INDEST-AICTE Consortium

The Indian National Digital Library in Engineering Sciences and Technology Consortium was setup in 2003 by the Ministry of Human Resource Development (MHRD). The consortium was renamed as INDEST-AICTE Consortium in December 2005 with AICTE playing a pivotal role enrolling its approved engineering colleges and institutions as members of the consortium for selected e-resources at much lower rates of subscription.

Objectives: 1. To provide electronic resources for the centrally funded and other academic institutions in Engineering, Science and Technology of India at highly subsidized rates. 2. To support and impart training to the users and librarians in the member institutions. 3. To improve scientific productivity of member institutions in terms of quality and quantity of publications.

ICSSR, New Delhi

In order to better utilization of research findings for policy planning purposes, an autonomous national organization known as the Indian Council of Social Science Research (ICSSR) was setup in 1969 on the recommendations of a Committee under the Chairmanship of Prof. V. K. R. V. Rao, the then Member of Planning Commission, in charge of Education. The ICSSR provides financial assistance to social sconce research centers and institutes, which are not affiliated or constituent organs of statutory universities.

ICSSR Regional Centres

In order to strengthen the activities of research institutes, the ICSSR, New Delhi, established regional Centres: 1. Western Regional Centre, Bombay (1973), covering Gujarat, Maharashtra, Goa, Dadra and Nagar Haveli, 2. Southern Regional Centre, Hyderabad (1973) covering Andhra Pradesh, Karnataka, Kerala, Tamil Nadu, Lakshadweep and Pondicherry, 3. Eastern Regional Centre, Calcutta (1973) covering Bihar, Orissa, Sikkim, Tripura, West Bengal and Andaman and Nicobar Islands, 4. North-Eastern Regional Center, Shillong (1977) covering Aurnachal Pradesh, Assam, Meghalaya, Manipur, Mizoram and Nagaland, 5. Northern Regional Centre, New Delhi covering Madhya Pradesh, Rajasthan, Uttar Pradesh and Delhi, 6. North Western Regional Centre, Chandigarh, covering Haryana, Himachal Pradesh, Jammu and Kashmir, Panjab and Chandigarh.

ICT Literacy

It is considered as the necessary skill required to use ICT to perform day-to-day professional work. It enables library professionals to use digital information resources effectively in their place of work.

ICT Skills

Include such as dexterity in operating systems, use of application software packages, knowledge of databases and programming, acquaintance in webpage design, library automation software, technical skills and managerial skills.

ILMS

It stands for Integrated Library Management Software developed and made available on DOS and UNIX Platforms. It is public domain library software of INFLIBNET. Training for handling the software was usually provided by software development and found sufficient for the staff at the level of college library. However INSDOC, DRTC and INFLIBNET had provided training to the staff of various institutions on payment relating to computers and different library maintenance softwares particularly CDS / ISIS.

INDEST (Indian National Digital Library in Science and Technology)

This was setup by Government of India, Ministry of Human Resource Development, New Delhi in December 2002. This is a consortium based subscription to electronic resources for technical education system in India.

INELI (International Network of Emerging Library Innovators)

It is a global public library leadership capacity building programme. It is working across seven regions of world viz. ASEAN, Balkans, India and South Asia, Latin America, Middle East and North Africa, Oceania and Suib-Saharan Africa. It is primarily funded and supported by the Global Libraries initiatives of the Bill & Melinda Gates Foundation (BMGF). The Global Libraries initiative is working for making public libraries relevant and vibrant information and community centres.

INFLIBNET

UGC has created a Network called Information and Library Network popularly known as INFLIBNET in the year 1991. It is an autonomous Inter-University Centre (IUC) in creating the infrastructure for sharing of library and information resources and services among academic and research institutions in India. It works jointly with University Libraries in India to shape the destiny of academic libraries in the formation of information environment in the country. It is a multiple service network that offers catalogue based services, database services, document delivery services, collection development and communication services.

Objectives : 1. To modernize libraries / Information Centres in the Country, 2. To establish a mechanism for information transfer and access to support scholarship and academic work, 3. To facilitate pooling, sharing optimization of library / information resources, 4. To organize library services at macro-level, at affordable cost and maximize benefits and 5. To provide speedy and efficient services to end users.

INID Codes

INID stands for Internationally agreed Numbers for the identification of (bibliographical) Data. These codes were standardized by the Paris Union Committee for International Cooperation in Information REtrieval among PATent Offices (ICIREPAT) under the auspices of the WIPO. The INSD Codes help in identifying the different data elements in patent document.

INID Codes are code numbers given to bibliographical data elements that are present on various pages of a patent document. The codes are primarily meant for the easy and accurate identification of bibliographic data appearing in a patent document or in a patent Gazette whatever be the language of origin.

ISDN

It is a set of international communication standards for transmitting voice, video, text, images and data simultaneously as digital signals over twisted pair telephone lines. The prime benefit of ISDN is speed. It allows people to send digital data ten times faster than the modern modems deliver on the analog voice network.

ISO 9000 Standards

These are a set of international quality management

standards and guidelines. The entire emphasis is on quality management and quality assurance, as part of the corporate philosophy and objectives, which in effect will be reflected in the performance of an organization. With the advent of ISO 9000 series of standards, it is now possible to measure tangibly the effectiveness of quality management in a information center. The objective of the ISO9000 series is to provide a mechanism for determining and fulfilling customer needs, preventing errors where possible.

ISO 9001 : 2000

International Standard Organization (ISO) located in Geneva is a World Wide Federation of National Standard Bodies, which are responsible for creating standards for each member country. ISO 9001 : 2000 is intended to be generic and applicable to all organizations, regardless of type, size and product category. One objective of the "Year 2000" revisions to the ISO 9000 family of standards is to simplify the structure and reduce the number of standards within the family. The replacement of ISO 9001 : 1994, ISO 9002 : 1994 and ISO 9003 : 1994 by a single quality management system (QMS) requirements standard, ISO 9001 : 2000 supports this Objective.

Benefits : 1. Customer Satisfaction, 2. Management Confidence, 3. Boosting employees morale, 4. Higher Productivity, 5. Higher acceptability, 6. Higher profitability and 7. Better access to global market.

Impact factor of a Journal

It is basically a ratio between citation and citable items published in a journal and indicate the relative standing and influence of the journal within its disciplinary boundaries. It is calculated by dividing the number of citations a journal receives for papers published during the latest two years by the number of articles this journal published during the same time.

Inclusive Library

An inclusive library provides facilities to everyone to participate in its programmes and get maximum benefit of the services being rendered to them. In addition an inclusive library intends to remove physical and attitudinal barriers that prevent patrons having disabilities from using the library, thus, it welcomes their participation in all library prorammes and services so that they are the beneficiaries of the library facilities to the maximum extent possible.

Index

It is an indicator or pointer, leading the user to the appropriate place of publication, where the information is available. It is designed to answer two queries – whether a particular piece of information is available and if so where it is located.

Indexing

The process of describing and identifying a document in terms of subject content. In the process of indexing, concepts are identified and extracted from documents by a process of analysis, then transcribed into the elements of the indexing tools, such as thesauri and classification schemes.

Indian Copyright Act, 1957

In India, the first legislation on Copyright was the Indian Copyright Act, 1847. It was passed by the then Governor General of India on December 18, 1847 on the lines of English Copyright Act, 1842 enacted British Parliament. In 1911 the law of Copyright was codified in England by Copyright Act, 1911. The Act applied all countries under British rule including India. Then the Governor General of India enacted Indian Copyright of 1914. After India's independence in 1947, the Indian Copyright Act, 1957 was enacted. This Act came into force on the 21st January, 1958 which was amended in 1961, 1984, 1992, 1994, 1999 and 2012.

Indian Council of Social Science Research (ICSSR)

This was set up in 1969 with the specific objective of promoting socio-economic research in the Country by establishing institutes and regional centers in the different parts of the Country funded jointly by the Central and State Governments, to support individual research projects and to provide research fellowships.

Indian Legal Deposit

In India two important Acts are in force, though not effectively, to achieve legal depost. These are: 1. Press and Registration of Books Act, 1867 (PR Act) and 2. Delivery of Books and Newspapers (Public Libraries) Act, 1954 (DB Act) including all of their amendments.

Indian National Bibliography (INB)

The Central Reference Library established in 1955 and located at the premises of National Library, Kolkata had been entrusted with the job of bringing out Indian National Bibliography (INB). It brings out current national bibliography of India on the basis of publications received by National Library, Kolkata, under the Delivery of Books and News Papers Act, 1954. The INB has been conceived as an authoritative and comprehensive bibliographical record of current Indian Publications in 15 major languages and are arranged ac cording classified sequence with an alphabetical Index. The entries provide full bibliographical details of listed publications. In order to facilitate bringing books of different languages under one sequence all entries are translated into Roman script with diacritical marks, whenever necessary. It is a monthly publication.

Indian National Scientific Documentation Centre (INSDOC)

It came into being in September 1951 and was engaged in providing S & T information and documentation services through myriad activities such as abstracting, indexing, design and development of databases, translation services, library automation, providing access to international information sources, human resource development, consultancy services in setting up modern library cum-information centres. INSDOC was also host to National Science Library and SAARC Documentation Centre. Prof. B. S. Kesavan was its first Director. This was merged in NISCAIR in 2002.

Indian Pharmacopoeia Commission (IPC)

IPC is an autonomous institution of the Ministry of Health and Family Welfare, Government of India. It was established to set standards of drugs in the country. Its basic function is to update regularly the standards of drugs commonly required for treatment of diseases prevailing in this region. It publishes official documents for improving quality of medicines by way of adding new and updating existing monographs in the form of I.P. It further promotes rational use of generic medicines by publishing National Formulary of India.

Industrial Information

It is much more wide-based and diverse in nature and quite different from scientific information. It covers the following: 1. Developmental information: Economic and social infrastructure, public service, energy, transport, power, education, training etc., 2. Managerial Information: Management, accounting, organizational cost analysis, production cost, financial problems, etc., 3. Marketing information: International and domestic competitors, export, import, in market, consumption, supply and demand, customers, marketing, etc., 4. Regulatory information: Industrial licensing policy, industrial law, company law, tax law, labour legislation, etc., 5. Technological information. Research and development, new products and processes, patents, technology import, appropriate technology, etc.

Information

1. It is any news, facts or data or knowledge derived or instructions gathered in any way. It is the product of different types of human activities and events or incidents expressed in the form of words, facts or data. It is made up of symbolic elements irrespective of their nature (numerical, textual, graphic etc.) and form of presentation (Paper, Print, microfilm or machine readable).

2. "It refers to facts and opinions provided and received during the course of daily life, one obtains information directly from other living beings, from mass media, from electronic data banks and from all sorts of observable phenomena in the surrounding environment" (New Encyclopedia Britannica, Vol.21).

3. "Information means – News or intelligence communicated by word or in writing, facts or data; knowledge derived from reading or instruction or gathered in any way" (New Webster's Dictionary)

Types of Information : 1. Conceptual, 2. Empirical, 3. Procedural, 4. Stimulatory, 5. Policy, and 6. Directive.

Need for Information : 1. To keep oneself current and competitive, 2. To discover new technologies / new concepts or researches, 3. To remain ahead in competition, 4. To capitalize on new markets, 5. To grow one's own business, 6. For problem solving, 7. For new ideas in any field, 8. For decision making , and 9, For developments.

Information Analysis Centre (IAC)

1. GS. Simpson Jr. was the first author to introduce the term 'Information Analysis Centre'. According to him "An IAC is a formally organized group of technical men for handling scientific and technical information in great depth within a narrow, well defined field in a timely and efficient manner, primarily for their peers".

2. According to E. Brady "An Information Analysis Centre is formally structured organizational unit specifically (but not necessarily exclusively) established for the purpose of acquiring, selecting, storing, retrieving, analyzing and synthesizing a body of information in a clearly defined specialized field or pertaining to a specialized mission with the intent of, compiling, digesting, repackaging or otherwise organizing and presenting pertinent information in a form of most authoritative, timely and useful to a society of peers and management".

Information Architecture

1. It means the way information is grouped, the navigation methods and terminology used within the system. It is commonly associated with websites and intranets, but it can be used in the context of any information structure or computer systems.
2. The art and science of organizing and labeling websites, intranets, online communities and software to support usability and findability.

Information Broker

He is an individual who provides information services on payment. Similar to a practicing doctor, advocate, chartered accountant. Practicing information professionals have emerged in a number of countries who charge from their clients for the services rendered to them. The client group may be from business, industry, government, academic or any other professional sector.

Information Brokering

"The services of information professionals or information research consultants world wise, who perform online searching, library research, competitor intelligence and similar services for business, industry, government, academic and the scientific communities. These knowledge workers charge for their expertise at locating, analyzing and / or interpreting information for use by a client" (Burwell Enterprise).

Information Communication Literacy

The necessary skills required to use the ICT to perform day-to-day professional work. It enables the library professionals to use digital information resources effectively in their place of work. This includes the use of ICT to perform routine professional work most efficiently and effectively including word processing, using spreadsheets, creating databases and presentations, manage networks, using Internet, performing automated activities, providing ICT based services, managing social and ethical issues in the library (M. A. Kamba).

Information Communication Technology (ICT)

1. It is considered as the fusion of computer technology and telecommunication technology.
2. "Diverse set of technological tools and resources used to communicate and to create, disseminate, store, and manage information".

Information Ecology

1. "The science of understanding and managing whole environment which include crises crossing relations among people, processes, support structures and the other elements of a company's information environment" (Davenport and Prusak)
2. "Information ecology is a term use to describe a persistent structure of people, practices and values in a particular local environment" (NardiO'Day).
3. "Information ecology is a science which studies the laws governing the influence of information summary on the

formation and functioning of bio-systems, including that of individuals, human communities and humanity in general and on the health and psychological, physical and social wellbeing of the human being, and which undertakes to develop methodologies to improve the information environment" (Online Wikipedia).

Attributes: 1. Information ecology is a system, 2. Diversity, 3. Co-evolution and 4. Keystone Species: Locality.

Information ethics

It is the branch of ethics that focuses on the relationship between the creation, organization, dissemination and use of information and the ethical standards and moral codes governing human conduct in society. It provides a critical framework for considering moral issues concerning information privacy, moral agency, new environmental issues and problem arising from life cycle.

Information Gathering

The process of accumulating, collecting, assembling and aggregation. The functions or acts are for the present and / or future use information.

Information hiding

It is a process of denying the free dissemination of information. When the information is ready for dissemination it is suppressed results in information siding. It is one kind of barrier to communication. In case of information hiding there may be a motive behind it. It is sometimes intentional hiding.

Resources: 1. Fear of losing authority, 2. Unintentional hiding, 3. Elimination of competitors, 4. Missing and 4. Delaying.

Information Industry

"Those industries in all countries which manufacture or create for the market information services or information products which can support individuals and organizations in doing the things with information that they need to do in order to achieve their work objective" (Elizabeth Orna). The information products generally maintained by the industry include discrete packages of information, developed prior to specific need for them.

Information Infrastructure

It means the national capabilities for making knowledge and information accessible for the transfer of knowledge and information and therefore putting knowledge to work. The components of information infrastructure are: a nucleus of physical information sources, a supply of required training manpower, linkages to significant decision making bodies, institutions, R&D establishments and technological institutions, two way communication channels with users, an organizational system that brings together and national policies that promote the systematic development of the infrastructure.

Information Literacy

The term Information Literacy was coined by Paul Zurkowski in 1974.

1. It is the ability of a person to locate, process and use information effectively regardless of delivery mechanism and the type of format in which the information appears in the global information society.
2. "It consists of skills, strategies and ways of thinking that are essential to success in a knowledge based economy. It is the ability to find and use information with critical discrimination in order to build knowledge. An information literate person is a lifelong learner, expert in using complex cognitive processes with diverse technological tools in order to solve problems in personal, social, economic and political contexts" (UNESCO).

3. "Information literacy is the set of skills needed to find, retrieve, analyze and use information.

Importance: 1. To be an independent lifelong learner, it is essential to achieve high level of information literacy, 2. To achieve equal opportunity among citizens, 3. To have critical thinking approach, 4. To realize strong and vibrant democracy, 5. To understand the copyright, 6 To minimize plagiarism.

Need for Information Literacy: 1. Rapid increase in the stream of information due to information revolution, 2. Advent of Information and Communication Technologies, 3. Vast variety of information sources, 4. Changing shape of libraries, 5. Wide dispersal of information, 5. Increase in the number of users and 6. Research on complex and inter-disciplinary topics.

Scope of Information Literacy:

1. *Traditional literacy*: To read and write,
2. *Computer literacy* : To understand and operate computers,
3. *Media literacy* : To understand different media storing networked information,
4. *Network Literacy*: Knowledge of networked information and skills to locate, select, evaluate and use of networked information,
5. *Visual literacy* : To see and understand the information and
6. *Web literacy* : To locate, select, retrieve and use information from the Web.

Benefit of Information Literacy : 1. Expansion of knowledge through substantive operations of knowledge creation, 2. Synthesis of data and information into knowledge, 3. Application of information and knowledge in problem solving, 4. Enhancement of critical thinking, 5. Motivation for self-directed learning and 6. Appreciation for lifelong learning.

Methods used for promotion of Information Literacy :

1. Lectures, 2. Seminars, Symposia and demonstrations, 3. Printed guides, books, newsletters, database user manual, 4. Audio-visual material like videotapes, film and audio-cassettes, 5. Individual instructions and 6. Online courses / tutorials.

Information Literacy Skills (ILS)

ILS are not skills which help students to only learn how to read and write but there are skills which help the students to be able to cope up with what we call "Information Age" or "Information Society" with more information.

Information Management (IM)

1. It is all about managing the processes of selection, collection, processing, controlling and dissemination of information in an organization. In Benner's opinion it (IM) helps an organization to recognize and use the potentials of the resources, information and information technology.
2. "The efficient and effective coordination of information from internal and external sources" (Cronin).
3. "Information Management is all about getting the right information, in the right form, to the right person, at the right cost, at the right time, in the right place, to take the right action". (Lynda Woodman).

Components : 1. Information sources including the identification, assessment and the use of both internal and external resources, 2. Technology, covering methods of inputting, storage, retrieving and distribution of information on both local and remote basis, 3. Management, involving strategic and business planning, human resource management, inter personal communication, accounting, budgeting and marketing.

Information Network (IN)

"A set of inter-related information systems associated with communication facilities, which are cooperating through more or less formal agreements in order to jointly implement information handling operations with a view to pooling their resources and to offer better services to the users. They generally follow identical or compatible rules and procedures" (UNISIST II working Document).

Objectives : 1. Promote sharing resources by inter-library loan, 2. Coordinate efforts for suitable collection development and reduce duplication, 3. Facilitate and promote delivery of documents electronically, 4. Establish referral centers to monitor and / or facilitate catalogue search, 5. Develops specialist bibliographic databases of books, serials and non-book materials, 6. Create databases for projects, specialists and institutions to provide online information service, 7. Implement computerization of operations and services in the libraries for faster communication of information, 8. Coordinate with other regional, national and international networks for exchange of information and documents, 9. Evolve standards and uniform guidelines in techniques, methods, procedures, hardware / software, services, etc. in order to facilitate sharing and exchange of resources.

Features : 1. Decentralized multilateral arrangement for flow of information, 2. Voluntary effort motivated by the desire to cooperate, 3. Planning of infrastructural facilities, 4. Linkage between information gatherers and users, 5. Greater access to information, 6. Oriented to user and 7. Economy.

Information Professions

This term designates all the specialized occupations which may be held by information specialists at various levels in relation to the handling or transfer of information, their study and teaching, e.g. archivists, librarians, document lists, information officers, information systems managers, information science teachers, etc., with various special qualifications.

Characteristics : 1. Development of a corpus of knowledge and derived techniques, 2. Provision of recognized professional training, 3. The existence of an association / associations, 4. Public recognition.

Information repackaging

A rearrangement of primary information obtained from various sources into tertiary information products or services tailored to the requirements of specific user group or individual user. The degree by transformation may vary from simple grouping to a full rewriting or transposition on a new medium e.g., audio-visual or a more accessible language according to the needs and characteristics of the users.

Information Resource Management (IRM)

It is the management (planning, organization and control) of the resources (human and physical) concerned with the systems support (development, enhancement and maintenance) and the servicing (Processing, transformation, distribution, storage and retrieval) of information (data, text) for an enterprise. It draws on the techniques of Information Science (Libraries) and Information systems (IT) related.

Information Retrieval (IR)

1. "The technique and process of searching, recovery and interpreting information from a large amount of stored data" (McGraw Hill Dictionary).
2. "Information retrieval is a system of locating facts in a central information storage area" (World Book Encyclopedia).
3. "Information retrieval is concerned with the structure, analysis, organization, storage, searching and

dissemination of information" (Encyclopedia of Computer Science).

Information Retrieval Thesaurus

It is a terminological control device for transformation of natural language expressions used by the authors, referees, publishers, indexers and users who form various links in the information transfer chain into a more constrained system vocabulary.

Information Science

1. "A discipline which investigates the characteristics of information and nature of information process, whilst not losing sight of the practical aspects of collecting, collating and evaluating information and its dissemination through appropriate intellectual apparatus and technology" (International Encyclopedia of Information and Library Science).

2. "Information Science is concerned with generation, collection, organization, interpretation, storage, retrieval, dissemination, transformation and use of information, with particular emphasis on the applications of modern technologies in these areas.

As a discipline, it seeks to create and structure a body of scientific, technological and systems knowledge related to transfer of information. It has both pure science (theoretical) components, which require into the subject without regard to application, and applied science (Practical) components, which develop services and products" (Brian Vickery).

Information Searching Behavior

1. It is the micro level behavior employed by the searcher in interacting with information systems of all kinds, it may be a human and computer interaction (Use of the mouse and clicks on links) or at the intellectual level involve mental acts such as judging the relevance of data

or information retrieved.
2. It is an individual requirement of resolute information which is searched, evaluated and use by him to satisfy her / his urge to know and updating of knowledge (S. B. Thiyan and N. Dlamini)
3. It is mainly concerned with who needs what kind of information and for what reasons, how information's found, evaluated and used and how their needs can be identified and satisfied. The process which takes place in the information seeking behavior are: 1. Identifying objective, 2. Define need, 3. Accessing information system, 4. Establishing sources of information, 5. Information acquisition, 6. Use of information and 7. Satisfaction / Dissatisfaction.

Information Security

It includes issues such as information management, information privacy and data integrity. Information security in a library would include personnel security and policies, steps taken for effective backups and the physical integrity of computing facilities. The security concept can be considered as the protection of data against accidental or international disclosure of unauthorized persons or unauthorized modifications or destruction.

Information Security Management

It describes controls that a library needs to implement to protect information assets from all potential threats to ensure the confidentiality, integrity and availability of information resources and help to identify and reduce critical security risks and types of network attacks for proper management of information security in digital libraries.

Information Seeking

It is the process of collecting and receiving information by different means. The means may include published or unpublished documents, communicating with colleagues, communication with peers, communicating with librarians, etc.

Information Seeking Behaviour (ISB)
1. It is broadly defined "as the field of studies that are concerned with who needs what kind of information and for what reasons; how information is found, evaluated and used, and how these needs can be identified and satisfied" (E. Auster).
2. "The complex patterns of actions and interactions that people engage in when seeking information of whatever kind for whatever purpose" (D. Ellis).
3. It is the purposive seeking for information as a consequence of a need to satisfy some goal. In the course of seeking the individual may interact with manual information systems such as a newspaper or library or with computer-based systems such as the Web.

Information Service Professionals
It refers to the whole group of professionals engaged in collecting information, their technical and physical processing and their storage, for the purpose of generating information dissemination and retrieval products and services, in order to satisfy information needs of those who are obliged to use information for discharging their duties and responsibilities.

Information Society
1. "A Society in which the quality of life as well as prospects for social change and economic development depend increasingly upon information and its exploitation. In such a society, living standards, patterns of work and leisure, the education system and the marketplace are all influenced markedly by advances in information and knowledge. This is evident by an increasing array of information – intensive products and services,

communicated through a wide range of media, many of them electronic in nature" (J. Martin).

2. "It is a society where the majority of people are engaged in creating, gathering, storage, processing and distribution of information" (Brans Comb).

Attributes : 1. Shift from an industrial economy to an information economy, 2. A tele-communication based information service infrastructure, 3. A high degree of computerization, large volume of electronic data transmission and adoption of Information technology, and 4. Rapid and convenient delivery of required information.

Characteristics of Information Era : 1. Dominant technology of the era is computer, 2. Icon of the era is microprocessor, 3. Science of the era is Computer Science, 4. Output of the era is knowledge, 5. Basis for wealth is information, 6. Defining work is knowledge worker, 7. Organizational structure is based on horizontal and networks, 8. Means of moving things is communication networks.

Information Sources

Physical origin of the information or place where it can be found. It may be a person, an institution or a document. Sources may be primary, secondary or tertiary according to the nature of information delivered.

Information System

1. "Information System is an organized procedure for collecting, processing, storing and retrieving information to satisfy a variety of needs" (Harrod's Librarians Glossary).

2. To define Information System, C. M. Brown identified four different components viz: "The first is a store of useful information which has been accumulated over a period of time. The second is a series of techniques which are used for adding material to and retrieving

information from the store upon demand. The third is a group of people who operate the system.... Finally the fourth component of an information system is the user. The ultimate test of any such system is the degree of satisfaction which it gives the user who has specific information need".

Objectives: 1. To explain how filtering data can provide information, 2. To identify and describe the major ways the monitoring method can be implemented, 3. To show how information can be used to highest key performance activities and identify potential opportunities, 4. To introduce the use of logic-mathematical models as a method for proving information to decision makers, 5. To illustrate based on interrogative method, how information is provided and 6. To develop and awareness for the use of information reflecting event and activities.

Information Technology (IT)

1. "As all resources of technology decisive to the processing, preserving and transmitting information in electronic form and the resources include computer, communication equipment and networks, fax machines and electronic, pocket calculator" (A. O. S. EmuakPor)

2. "Scientific, Technological and engineering disciplines and the management techniques use in information handling and processing; their applications; computers and their interactions with men and machines and associated social, economic and cultural matters" (UNESCO).

3. "Various means of obtaining, storing and transferring information using computers, telecommunication and microelectronics" (Moll).

Objectives: 1. To support technical functions associated with technical processing and circulation work, 2. To support information storage, retrieval and dissemination systems, 3.

To support management information services for librarians, 4. To be best used in service and orientation courses for working librarians, continuing education programmes for LIS teachers, distance education programmes, etc.

Components: 1. Processor, memory and input/output channels, 2. Micro, mini and super computers, 3. Mass storage technologies, 4. Data communication, networking and distributed processing, 5. Data entry, display response and 6. Software. **The new I.T. can be grouped into four major areas such as:** 1. Computer technology, 2. Telecommunication technology, 3. Reprographic technology and 4. Satellite technology.

Information Therapy

According to Kemper it is "Prescribing evidence based right information to the right patient at the right time to help them make medical decisions and improve a self-management behavior".

Concepts: Right information, Right person and Right time. It is a latest approach in health and medical sciences that changes the role of information from being about care to being a part of care.

Information Transfer

A set of successive operations, by which knowledge is made available to different categories of users after its initial generation by producers. It includes the production i.e. recording of primary, secondary and tertiary information, the production of corresponding documents, their distribution, storage, processing, dissemination, their search, access and exposition, through all possible channels. (UNISIST Document).

Information use behaviour

It consists of the physical and mental acts involved in incorporating the information found into the person's existing knowledge base. It may involve, therefore, physical acts such as marking sections in a text to note their importance or significance, as well as mental acts involved, for example, comparison of new information with existing knowledge.

Informetrics

1. "The matric discipline concerned with the study of mathematical and statistical methods and models and their application to the quantitative analysis of the structure and properties of scientific information and the patterns and laws of scientific communication process including identification of laws proper". (M. Morales). The term 'informetrics' was first proposed by Otto Nacke of West Germany in 1979.
2. "Informetrics is the study of the quantitative aspects of information in any form, not just records or bibliographies and in any social group, not just scientists" (Tague-Sutcliffe).
3. Informetrics is the quantitative study of collections of moderate-sized units of potentially informative text, directed to the scientific understanding of informing process at the social level" (Wilson).

Infrastructure as a Service

It delivers computer infrastructure i.e. a platform virtualization environment as a service along with raw (block) storage and networking. In this rather than purchasing services, software, data centre space or network equipment, clients, instead buy those resources as a fully outsourced service.

Institutional Archive (IA)

An Institutional archive may be defined as an online locus for collecting and preserving in digital form – the intellectual output of an institution, particularly a research institution (Wikipedia). In other words IA is a collection of digital research documents, such as articles, book chapters, conference papers and data sets. E-prints are the digital texts of peer-reviewed research articles before and after refereeing.

Objectives : 1. To create global visibility for an institution's scholarly research, 2. To collect content in single location, 3. To provide access to institutional research output by self-archiving and 4. To store and preserve other institutional digital assets.

Institutional Repository

1. A digital collection maintained by the University or an academic institution to capture and preserve the intellectual output of its staff and faculty members is called an institutional repository.

2. A set of services that a university offers to the members of its community for the management and dissemination of digital material created by the institutions and its community members. It is most essentially an organizational commitment to the stewardship of these digital materials including long-term preservation where appropriate as well as organization and access or distribution (P. Gosetti).

3. "A web based database (repository) of scholarly material which is institutionally defined (as opposed to subject-based repository) cumulative and perpetual (a collection of record) open and inter operable (e.g.: using OA1-compliant software) and thus collects stores and disseminates. In addition most would include long-term preservation of digital materials as a key function of IRS" (Mark Ware).

Objectives : 1. To provide open access to institutional research output by self-archiving it, 2. To create global visibility for an institution scholarly research, 3. To collect content in a single location, 4. To store and preserve the other institutional digital assets including unpublished or otherwise easily lost

(Gray) literature.

Importance: 1. Expansion of the range of knowledge that can be shared, 2. Opportunities to simplify and extend dissemination, 3. Highlighting of the quality of intellectual output and 4. Opportunities for new forms of scholarly communication.

Drawbacks: 1. Effect the balance of institutional power as some departments proceed faster than others, 2. They rely on unproven methods for long-term digital preservation and 3. Initial costs may be high as contributors perceive high risks and duplicate effort to reduce them". (Yeates).

Benefits: 1. Enhanced research capacity, 2. Avoidance of duplication, 2. Raise of status of Institute and its image, 4. Managing Institutional information assets, 5. Long-term cost saving, 6. Easy dissemination of information, 7. Highlighting the quality of intellectual capital, 8. Opportunities for new forms of scholarly communication, and 9. Flexible ways to develop existing scholarly communication.

Intellectual Property (IP)

It means the legal rights which result from intellectual activity in the industrial, scientific, literary and artistic fields. It relates to items of information or knowledge, which can be incorporated in tangible objects at the same time in an unlimited number of copies at different locations anywhere in the world. The property is not in the copies but in the information or knowledge reflected in them.

Intellectual Property Rights (IPR)

1. It means "natural rights to protect his / her works or intellectual property as well as to control over all possible means of reproducing his / her works by others and secondly the transfer or dissemination of his / her ideas to the target user without interruption" (N.J. Bamane).
2. World Intellectual Property Organization (WIPO)

defines Intellectual Property in a broad sense. According to this definition IP shall include the rights relating to: "1. *Literacy, artistic and scientific works;* 2. *Performances of performing artists, phonograms and broadcasts,* 3. *Inventions in all fields of human endeavor,* 4. *Scientific discoveries,* 5. *Industrial designs,* 6. *Trademarks, service marks, and commercial names and designations.,* and 7. *Protection against unfair competition and all other rights resulting from intellectual activity in the industrial, scientific, literacy or artistic fields.*

International Nuclear Information System (INIS)

The International Nuclear Information System (INIS) of the International Atomic Energy Agency (IAEA), Vienna is the most sophisticated and comprehensive information system in the field of nuclear science and technology. Its bibliographic database is created with the active participation of 65 member states and 13 international agencies which scan and input the bibliographic information of all nuclear literature falling within the specified subject – scope of INIS and published in their respective geographic regions. The bibliographic database follows a number of international standards for its content and structure making compatible with most of the computer based data I. R. Systems acceptable to national information centres in the world to provide a wide range of information dissemination services.

INIS in India : The Library and Information Services (L&IS) of Bhabha Atomic Research Centre (BARC), Bombay (Mumbai) is responsible for all activities connected with INIS in India.

International Organization for Standardization (ISO)

At the International level, the principal organization responsible for development of technical standards is International Organization for Standardization (ISO) headquarters at Geneva. It was founded in 1946 by 25 national standards associations to carry on the work of the International Federation of the National Standardizing Associations which was originally organized in 1920. ISO is a non-governmental organization.

ISO Technical Committee (TC) is TC46 titled Information and Documentation which is concerned with Library and Information Science. The scope of TC46 is standardization practices relation to libraries, documentation and information centres, indexing and abstracting services, archives, information science and publishing.

International Patent Classification (IPC)

The IPC was developed by the World Intellectual Property Organization (WIPO) to serve as common classification system for patents issued by various patent offices all over the world. The IPC system was a result of international cooperative effort by the Industrial property offices of many countries. The Strasbourg agreement of 1970 concerning the IPC, which came into force on October 7, 1975 provides for common classification for products, inventions, inventor's certificates and utility models. The administration of IPC is the sole responsibility of the WIPO.

International Standard Book Number (ISBN)

ISBN is a unique number given to a book by one specific publisher to identify its publisher, the individual title or a volume of a multi-volume book and its unique to that title or edition or volume. The Standard Book Number consists of 10 digits with four subparts viz.

1. Group / Country Identifier (GI),
2. Publisher's Identifier (PI) also called publisher's prefix,
3. Title Identifier (TI),
4. Check Digit (CD) Example: ISBN--*81-200-0001-3* (GI) (PI) (TI) (CD)

The Publisher Identifier shall be assigned by the Centre and the number of digits representing a publisher will vary depending upon the output of titles of the assigned publisher. Likewise, the title identifier for the individual titles shall be allocated by the publisher from the list of readymade numbers supplied by the Centre. The fourth part which is 10 the digit will be the check digit. This number is computed as a result of an elaborate calculation on other nine digits.

Internet

It is the networking of computer networks around the world which facilitates transfer of sharing of information among all computer users connected to these networks. Internet is a World Wide Communication System which links together thousands of computers. It is a network of thousands of networks which communicate among the members using a single set of software which are generally known as protocols. The protocols make sure of connectivity to the right computer to interact. Internet provides inter-connectivity between government agencies, educational institutions, libraries, companies, individuals or anybody who has personal computer system.

Features: 1. Enables worldwide search, 2. Enables large volume of communication, 3. Low cost operation and maintenance, 4. Open standards and few rules, 5. Interactive nature, and 6. Support for multimedia information exchange.

Few common facilities offered by Internet: 1. Access to data stored in remote computers, 2. Access to wide selection of public domain and shareware software, 3. Exchange of electronic mail and other data files in a wide area environment, 4. On real-time interaction with other network users, 5. Receipt and delivery of electronic publications, 6. Participation in electronic media mailing lists and conferences, 7. Access to remote scientific commuting equipment such as super-computers, remote sensing equipment, telescopes and graphic processors.

Impact : 1. Better, faster, timelier communication with colleagues and sources of information, 2. Enhanced collaboration, 3. Better dissemination of information, 4. Reduction in barriers to publication, 5. Access to public databases, 6. Free access to abstracts and / or tables of contents of periodical literature.

Internet Bookshops

These are online bookshops that allow the user community to search the items of its interest, navigate, make a query, communicate, place an order, bargain and negotiate. Simply the Internet Bookshop or online Bookshop list the products for sale or the services offered and invite customer to phone, fax or e-mail their order.

Advantages : 1. Provide access to information to any one at anytime from anywhere, 2. One can make his / her time searching for books at any time i.e. day or night, 3. Online bookstores allow one to view a lot of books at one time, 4. These are just databases – repositories of vast amount of information about books currently on the market, 4. Online bookstores are convenient for scholars and other looking for specific titles, 5. Published lists of books can be accessed through internet.

Internet of Things (IoT)

It is basically a network of several devices which are attached with miscellaneous software, electronics, and network connectivity of district orientations aimed at exchanging and compiling of any kind of information. IoT in general is applied in many industries including finance, travel, teaching, telecommunication, etc.

Internship in a Library

"It is a period of supervised experience specifically designed to give the trained but inexperienced librarian a well-rounded working view of the field. It reaches this goal by varied assignments throughout the library by formal and informal discussion of the specific tasks, the reasons for the work, the methods chosen and by providing for the study of the fundamental component of the library, its literature" (E. Broadman).

Attributes: 1. It is a post-course programme, 2. It is to be taken on full-time basis, 3. It is to be supervised by the staff of the host library and teaching faculty of LIS Departments, and 4. It serves as a link between pre-service education and placement experience.

Advantages : 1. It provides real-life experience of handling the library operations and attending to the guidance from senior professionals, 2. It helps in confidence building on the interns in their professional jobs in library situations, 3. It helps in career building among interns, 4. It creates motivations among the budding professionals to take up the library profession, 5. It helps to get practical experience and certificate the intern gets from the institution helps in getting proper placements, 6. It helps in learning the state of art of technology applied in the subject field and 7. It helps the internees to learn the work culture and how to deal with the library clients.

Interoperability

1. It is the ability of diverse systems and organizations to work together. The term is usually used in technical systems engineering sense or alternatively in a broad sense, taking into account social, political and organizational factors that impact system performance.
2. "The ability of two or more systems or components to exchange information and use the exchanged information without special effort on either system" (ALCTS 2004).
3. "The ability of two or more systems such that they can exchange information and data without any special manipulating" (Taylor 2004).

Invisible Colleges

De Solla Price first coined the phrase 'Invisible Colleges'. It is the information communication among knowledgeable sources. It is the information transfer process that exists between scientists and researchers for more personally and regularly using informal channels like letters, telephone and personal meetings. Such informal communication patterns exist between scientists and have an important role in the transmission of information as it is a crucial and at the forefront of research arena.

Invisible Water Marking

In this process information is added as digital data to audio, picture or video, but cannot be perceived as such. An important application of invisible water marking is to copyright protection systems which are intended to prevent or deter unauthorized copying of digital media.

J

JCCC@INFONET

J. Gate custom content for consortium (JCCC) which is a virtual library of journal literature created as customized e-journals access gateway and database solution for the UGC-INFONET Digital Library Consortium. It acts as one-point access to journals that are available on-line and subscribed by the consortium as well as 22 University Libraries that are designated as ILL Centres (Inter Library Lending Centres).

Job Analysis

"It is the process of studying and collecting information relating to operations and responsibilities of a specific job". It includes: 1. Identification of the specific activities performed in a job, 2. Characteristics of a person, 3. Work situation and 4.

Material and equipment necessary for performing the job effectively.

Job Description

It is an organized, factual statement of the duties and responsibilities of a specific job. In brief it should tell what is to be done, how it is done and why. It is a standard function, in that defines the appropriate and authorized content of a job.

Job Evaluation

It is a systematic and orderly process of determining the worth of a job in relation to other jobs. The objective of this process is to determine the correct rate of pay. It is not the same as job analysis. Rather it should follow the job analysis process, which provides the basic data to be evaluated.

Job Specification

It is a statement of the minimum acceptable human qualities necessary to perform a job properly. In contrast to the job description, it is a standard of personnel and designates the qualities required for acceptable performance.

Job Psychograph

It consists of a complete statement of the personnel requirements for a job and job psychograph involves an analysis and specification of special abilities necessary for success of a particular job. It is an analysis in terms of the abilities required to do the job. In job psychograph a list of traits like proficiency, alertness, imitative from different areas is presented and each trait is rates on five point scale in accordance with its degrees of importance for a particular job in question by a person familiar with the job.

Job Satisfaction

It refers to feelings and emotional aspects of the individuals experience towards his job as different from intellectual or rational aspects. It refers to a person's feeling of satisfaction on the job which acts as a motivation to work. Some definitions are as follows:

1. "Any combination of psychological, physiological and environmental circumstances that causes a person truthfully to say I am satisfied with my job" (R. Hoppock).
2. "Job satisfaction a function of the perceived characteristics of a job in relation to an individual's frame of reference" (P. C. Smith).
3. "As a pleasurable or positive emotional state resulting from appraisal of job and job experience" (E. A. Locke).

Determinants of Job Satisfaction : 1. Style of Supervision, 2. Work itself, 3. Congenial working environments, 4. Pay, 5. Promotion, 6. Co-workers, 7. Job Security and 8. Opportunity for advancement.

Joomla!

Joomla! Is an open source content management system platform for publishing content on the World Wide Web and intranets. It is written in PHP, stores data in My SQL and includes features such as page caching, RSS feeds, printable versions of pages, news flashes, blogs, polls, search and support for language internationalization.

Features : 1. Page catering to improve performance, 2. RSS leads, 3. Printable versions of pages, 4. News flashes, 5. Blogs, 6. Polls, 7. Website searching and 8. Language internationalization.

Journal

"A journal is a periodical especially one containing scholarly article and / or disseminating current information on research and development in a particular subject field. If the task is done by electronic media, then it may be called e-journals. If the content of the journal produced, stored and scanned in a database and then retrieved online, then the same is called online journal" (ALA Glossary, 1983).

Journal of Intellectual Property Rights (JIPR)

It is a peer reviewed bimonthly journal started in 1986 by CSIR – National Institute of Science Communication and Information Resources (CSIR-NICAIR), New Delhi. It was the first journal in the area of IPR from India. Its objectives are: 1. To enhance IPR related communication among policy makers, organizational agents, academics and managers for critical understanding and research on intellectual properly and 2. To promote the development of newly cultivated research field.

Journal Packing Density (JPD)

It can be defined as "the average number of research articles published in each issue or each volume of a research journal".

Journals

These are considered as a very important channels communication especially among the researchers in the learned world for their R & D activities. These are considered as primary source to explore the new frontiers of knowledge. There are large number of journals published in almost every subject, field including Library and Information (LIS) in India.

K

KOHA

KOHA is the first open-source integrated library system (ILS) that was originally developed by Kapto communications limited, New Zealand for the Horowhenua Library Trust in 1999. KOHA was released as free software under general public license in 2000. It supports all modules of library applications as well as has support for Z39.50 server as MARC-21 / UNIMARC, IAI-PMH, ISO-2709 and also supports several next generation OPAC features.

Key Features: 1. Full-featured ILS, 2. Library Standards Complaint, 3. Web based interfaces, 4. Free software, 5. No Vendor Lock in, 6. Active development process, 7. Frequent software releases.

KOHA Live CD

It contains Linux operating system and installed instance of Koha Library Management System. Koha package is pre-installed in the CD and ready to use after installation of live CD. It allows library professionals to test the software before tacking decision on KOHA implementation.

Benefits: 1. Bundled with Linux Operating System, 2. Suitable for trial without installation inside the hard disk of the computer, 3 User friendly installations, 4. Customer version of KOHA is ready for use, 5. Suitable for offline installation and no need of internet connection for installation.

KOPAL

It is a cooperative development of long-term digital archive of German National Library and Universities Bibliothek, Gottingen. The goal of this project is to develop a technical, organizational solution to ensure long-term availability of electronic resources. It preserves bit streams and digital documents follows three steps of storage, migration and emulation.

Kalasampada

It is a digital repository developed by Cultural Informatics Library (CIL) Unit of IGNCA established in 1994 with the assistance of UNDP. The project aims to use multimedia computer technology to develop software package that integrates a variety of cultural information and helps the user community to interact and explore the subject available in image, audio, text, graphics animation and video on a computer. The Kalasampada facilitates the user to access and view the material from over 100,000 manuscripts, over 100,000 slides, rae books thousands of rare photographs, audio and vieo along with highly researched publications of the INGCA from a single computer interface.

Keywords

These provide readers with suitable terms to use in web-based searches to locate other materials on similar topics. Keywords also enable indexers and editors to retrieve related materials. Keywords indicate growth of a subject in different orientations but the notable feature is that the selection of keywords is a vital aspect. Keywords occur within titles, abstracts, series names, content-notes, subject-headings and index terms provided by the authors. These may also be used as effective subject access points.

Keyword Classification

A Keyword Classification is the automatic construction of classification schemes through an examination of keywords used in indexing documents. Its primary objective is not to cluster the document collection but to derive grouping keywords. Keyword classification can be used to characterize the document in a collection as an aid to retrieval.

Kisan Call Centre (KCC)

It consists of a complex of telecommunication infrastructure, computer support and human resources organized to manage effectively and efficiently the queries raised by farmers instantly in local languages. Mainly Subject Matter Specialists (SMSs) using telephone and computer interact with farmers to understand the problems and answer the queries at a Kisan Call Centre.

The Dept. of Agriculture & Cooperation, Ministry of Agriculture, Govt. of India launched KCCs on 21st

January, 2004.

Knowledge

1. It is the "full utilization of information and data, coupled with potential of people's skills, competencies, ideas, intuitions, commitments and motivations" (D. Gray).
2. "The totality of ideas conserved y he humans. In this sense knowledge is equal to the universe of ideas" (S R. Ranganathan).
3. "The fact or condition of knowing something with familiarity gained through experience or association" (Webster's New Collegiate Dictionary).
4. Knowledge is fluid mix of framed experience, values, contextual information and expert insight that provides frame work for evaluating and incorporating new experience and information. It originates and is applied in the minds of knower. In organizations, it often becomes embedded not only documents or repositories but also in organizational routines, processes, practices and norms" (Davenport and Prusak).

Characteristics: 1. Infinite, 2. Continuum, 3. Turbulently dynamic, 4. Manifold and multidimensional, 5. Cumulative, 6. Coherent and 7. Multidirectional.

Knowledge Audit

It is a planning document which provides structural overview of an organization's knowledge in a designated section or target area. Audit document gives a qualitative and quantitative view of the individual chunks of knowledge stored in repositories. Knowledge repositories could be electronic (databases), Paper based (files) or Individuals (Experts).

Knowledge Integration

It is the capacities to transform an organization's

knowledge resources (tacit, explicit, individual, organizational, internal and external) into actionable knowledge by taking into account the organization's strengths, weaknesses and opportunities as well as threats to the organization.

Knowledge Management (KM)

1. It is the process of transforming information and intellectual assets into enduring value. It connects people with the knowledge that they need to take action. In corporate sector managing knowledge is considered as a key to achieve breakthrough and competitive advantage.

2. "Knowledge management covers: Identifying what knowledge assets accompany possesses, analyzing how the knowledge can add value, specifying what actions are necessary to achieve better usability and added value, and reviewing the use of knowledge to ensure added value". (Liebowitz and Beckman).

Strategies: 1. K.E.S. Veiley listed the following strategies for KM.

These are: 1. Transferring information and best practices via I.T. Systems, 2. Capturing about customers, 3. Leveraging R & D into several applications, 4. Creating more value from existing intellectual assets, 5. Creating strategy focused on individuals innovation and knowledge creation and 6. Commitment to knowledge focused strategy.

Technologies : 1. Web Technologies, 2. Training, 3. Systems, 4. Communication, 5. Artificial Intelligence, 6. Advice, 7. Knowledge discerning.

Knowledge Management (KM) Strategy

It is a plan that described how an organization will manage its knowledge better for the benefit of that organization and its users. A good knowledge management strategy is closely aligned with the organizations overall strategy objectives (BeenacheruKuth). There are two types of knowledge strategies for sharing and managing knowledge in the organization viz. 1. Codification Strategy and 2. Personalization Strategy.

Knowledge Mapping

It consists of survey, audit and synthesis. It aims to track the acquisition and loss of information and knowledge. It explores personal and group competencies and proficiencies. It illustrates or maps how knowledge flows throughout an organization.

Knowledge Organization (KO), 1974

Formerly International Classification has been serving as a common platform for the discussion of both theoretical background questions and practical application problems in many areas of concern. The contributions of experts deal with: "1. Clarifying theoretical foundations, 2. Describing practical operations connected with numerical taxonomy / classification, as well as application of classification systems and thesauri, manual and machine indexing, 3. Tracing the history of classification knowledge and methodology, 4. Discussing questions of education and training in classification, 5. Concerning themselves with the problems of terminology in general and with respect to special fields". This journal is the organ of International Society for Knowledge Organization (ISKO), Frankfurt.

Knowledge Organization (KO)

According to Dr. I. Dahlerg Knowledge Organisation encompasses the follow:
1. The epistemological, mathematical, system-theoretical cognitive scientific and scientific theoretical premises of order of concepts as well as their historical background.

2. The knowledge of elements and structures of systems of concepts.
3. The methodology of construction, conservation, revision and evaluation of this system.
4. The methodology of intellectual and machine applications of this system via classification and indexing,.
5. Special taxonomies and classification systems including documentation language (thesauri).
6. Questions arising from related areas such as linguistics and terminology, including the retrieval problems, especially online access.
7. The entire periphery of knowledge organization in the work place, individual centres, societies, countries and in international areas, as the question of education, the economy, the user, etc."

Knowledge Portal

It means a magical or technological doorway that connects two distant locations, it means a website considered as an entry point to other websites often by being or providing access to a search engine of the website.

Knowledge Sharing

It is a process of receiving and providing information, giving feedback after experiencing the use technology and product by the staff. It is the most influential factors comparable to other knowledge related behaviors. It is so important in academia as knowledge creation, integration and other related issues are directly influenced by it. (M.T Hansen).

Knowledge Society

A Knowledge Society has the characteristic that knowledge forms major component of any human activity. Human activities such as economic, social, cultural and all other activities become dependent on vast reservoir of knowledge and information. A knowledge society is one which knowledge becomes major creative force.

Kritisampada: The National Database of Manuscripts

National Mission for Manuscripts is the biggest and most ambitious project is to create a database of all Indian manuscripts in the country and abroad. The National Database of Manuscripts, Kritisampada, is available on the internet through the Mission's Website. It aims to document as far as possible, each manuscript whether in a museum, library, temple, madrassa or a private collection. The mission's biggest objective is to discover and document such manuscripts for posterity.

L

LAN (Local Area Network)

It is basically a transmission system for linking computers over a restricted geographical area. It is combination of cables / connectors, computers, processors and interface software which interconnects computers and related devices. It regulates the flow of information traffic among these devices.

LIBSYS

It is an targeted library management system developed by Lib.Sys Corporation, Gurgaon. It is the most popular library software in India and has been installed in more than 1000 different types of libraries. Lib.Sys provides full graphic user interface front end for the windows client. It is designed to run on various platforms like Windows (95/98 NT/2000/XP) UX, Linux, Novell, Lan etc. It is built around its own bibliographic databases allowing ANSI Z39.50 format and support variable field length for different types of documents. It works on a client-server environment and supports Unicode that facilities handling of both International and Indian languages. It needs traditional authorization (identification) to access various modules. There are six modules in the software, viz. acquisition system, circulation system, cataloguing system, serial system, OPAC and article indexing.

LIBWARE

The Union of Library Processes and Software support for retrieval of information is called as LIBWARE so as to distinguish it from either library procedure or software alone. Effective results can be derived when LIBWARE is carefully designed.

Characteristics : 1. Self-descriptiveness of a system, 2. User Control, 3. Ease of learning, 4. Correspondence with user expectations, 5. Flexibility in tasks handling and 6. Tolerance of user needs (W.Drida)

LOCKSS

The LOCKSS (Lots of Copies Keep Stuff Safe) programme stated by Stanford University Libraries is an open source digital preservation system. The participating libraries acquire digital content in their local LOCKSS Box. Through a LOCKSS distributed network, libraries cooperate with each other to ensure their preserved content remains authentic and authoritative. The LOCKSS delivers a copy of original publication to authorized users in real-time, whenever it is needed. At present LOCKSS has more than 9000 e-journal titles from 510 publications.

LEADERSHIP

1. "Leadership is the activity of influencing people to strive willingly for group objectives". (G. R. Terry).

   Style : "A style that maximizes productivity and

satisfaction, growth and development in all situations" (Blake).

Different Styles : 1 Telling, 2. Selling, 3. Participating, and 4. Delegating.

Qualities : 1. Power to listen, 2. Availability, 3. Tolerance, 4. Adaptability, 5. Discrimination, 6. Decision making, 7. Ability to respond and 8. Team Spirit.

2. "The ability to develop and share a vision of desired future and influence people to direct their energies towards achievement of desired mission, goals and objective"(N Christian).

Legal Deposit

1. I is a statutory obligation to ensure the preservation of entire intellectual output of a country for complete bibliographic control of its publication.
2. "The requirement, enforceable by law, to deposit with one or more specific agencies copies of publications of all kinds reproduced in any medium or with any process for public distribution, lease or sale" (Lunn).
3. Purpose: 1. It helps put copyright legislation into effect, 2. It ensures preservation of material being produced contemporaneously for posterity, 3. In some countries it acts as the signal for explicit authorization for the publication of the work deposited, 4. It helps to produce a comprehensive national bibliography. (A. R. Bandyopadhyay).

Lexicography and Onomantics

It is the science that undergirds the preparation of dictionaries as lists of words and phrases whose meanings are defined on the basis of semantic analysis. By contrast onomantics reverses this paradigm, it identified concepts that are related to each other and need to represent as important tools in the production and organization of knowledge.

Terminology bridges these two approaches, it draws heavily on the lexicographic model while moving stolidly toward an onomantic framework.(F. W.Riggs).

Librametry

The application of quantitative methods in the management of library and its services (S.R.Ranganathan). He was the first person who in the year 1948 suggested the term 'librametry' at ASLIB Conference in Leamington Spa (U.K.). Later three more terms viz: bibliometrics, scientometric, informetrics and now webometrics have been coined and being used.

Librarianship

"The profession concerned with application of knowledge of media and those principles and theories, techniques and technologies which contribute to the establishment, preservation, organization and utilization of collections of library material and to the dissemination of media" (ALA Glossary).

Library

1. "A Collection of books and other literary material kept for reading, study and consultation, 2. A place, building, room or rooms set apart for the keeping and use of a collection of books, 3. A collection of films, photographs and other visual non-book materials, plastic or metal tapes and discs, computer tapes and programs. All of these as well as printed and manuscript documents, may be provided in departments of one large library or they may be in collections restricted to one large library or they may be in collections restricted to one type of material" (The Librarians" Glossary and Reference Book).

Objectives Broadly : 1. To serve the needs of user community, 2. To provide reference and other reading materials to all user community, 3. To provide a lending service to different types of readers, 4. To provide effective ready and long-range reference and information services, 5. To give user community quick access to reliable information over the whole range of entire knowledge.

Functions Broadly: 1. The acquisition of both macro and micro publications to the user community, 2. The storage relevant documents of all types so that they can be retrieved for use, 3. Guidance to user community on the use of various collections and acquiring needed material from other libraries through resource sharing and networking, and 4. Conservation of reading materials by modern preservation methods, and 5. Offering various types of user services.

Library 2.0

It is about using new web technologies to connect and establish relationships with patrons. Web 2.0 is a term coined to describe the emerging internet technologies. Hence, the birth of the phrase "Library 2.0" to describe use of these new web applications within library systems.

It follows the principle of Web 2.0 in that it promotes the evaluation and adoption of software and tools which were originally created outside of the library environment. These are overlaid or traditional library services such as the library OPAC in order to create a more dynamic, interactive and personalized user experience.

Essential Elements : 1. User centered, 2. Provides multimedia experience, 3. It is socially rich and 4. It is community based innovative

Library and Information Security

It is a method which is being used to conserve and preserve the integrity, availability and confidentiality of electronic information. Security control reduced the impact or probability of security threats and vulnerabilities to a level acceptable to an organization or an institution.

Library Anxiety

Constance A. Mellon first used the term 'Library anxiety' to define students' mental state in using the library. It is an unpleasant feeling or emotional state with psychological and behavioral concomitants which comes in the fore in a library setting.

Library Automation

The application of information technology with an emphasis on advanced computers in the upkeep of library functions such as: Acquisition, processing (classification and cataloguing), circulation, periodical management, and other maintenance jobs viz: Stock verification, Binding, Loss of Books / CDs, reader's tickets, Reminders to members / vendors / binders, etc. may be termed as Library Automation.

1. Need : 1. To handle any amount of data and information, 2. To participate in network programmes and resource sharing, 3. To introduce flexibility in information searching, 4. To standardize library procedures, 5. To speedily process information and its retrieval, 6. To achieve better bibliographic control at all levels, 7. To overcome geographical barriers to communication and 8. To market library products and services.

2. Objectives : 1. To maintain bibliographical records of all materials in a computerized form, 2. To provide bibliographical details through a simple enumerative access point of holdings of a library, 3. To reduce the repetition in technical processes of housekeeping operations, 4. To provide access to information at a faster rate, 5. To share the resources through library networking, and 6. To implement new IT processes to provide quality information.

3. Advantages : 1. Improvement in the quality, speed and effectiveness of library functioning, 2. Relieving of professionals staff from routine work, 3. Libraries can reach wider users, 4. Facilitation for resource sharing and networking, 5. Efficient management of library resources, 6. Better and more utilization of resource's, 7. Various types of documents can be preserved for posterity through digitization and 8. Digitization makes rare documents available to scholars and researchers.

Areas of Library Automation: 1. Library housekeeping functions, 2. Information storage and retrieval, 3. Systems analysis and Operations Research, 4. Library Network Applications, and 5. Office Automation.

Library Collection

"Library collection is the sum total of library materials, books, manuscripts, serials, government documents, pamphlets, catalogues, reports, recordings, microfilm reels, microcards and microfiche, CDs etc., that make up the holding of a particular library" (Encyclopedia of Library and Information Science).

Library Consortia

1. It consists of number of libraries preferably with some homogeneous characteristics by subject, institutional affiliation or affiliation to funding authorities that come together with an objective to do certain jobs collectively. These include: *1. Subscription to e-resources, 2. Resource sharing, 3. Shared cataloguing of resources, 4. Shared technology solutions, 5. Shared core / peripheral collections and 6. Shared cataloguing in network environment.*

2. It is a group of two or more libraries that have agreed to cooperate with each other in order to fulfill certain similar needs, usually resource sharing. A consortium supports resource sharing and provided services to users through programmes in cooperative acquisition, access to electronic resources, access to physical

collections, enhanced inter-library loan and document delivery.

Need : 1. Difficulty in maintaining subscription of e-resources, 2. Increasing price hike, 3. Sharing fiscal provisions for libraries, 4. Exponential growth of library resources particularly e-journals, 5. Changing needs of user community, to access to their learned journals, 6. Rational utilization of library fund, 7. Wider access to a large pool of resources, 8. Reduction in staff strength, and 9. Better, faster and cheaper services.

Advantages of Library Consortia : 1. Enhanced Cooperation, 2. Augmentation of Resource base with less money, 3. Adoption of new technology for providing better services, 4. Rational use of library budget, 5. Sharing of professional expertise among member libraries, 6. Providing a platform for discussion and sharing of professional issues and problems, 7. Reducing unit cost of information, 8. Small libraries can derive more benefits out of their small budgets.

Disadvantages : 1. Initial investments on licenses and development of related infrastructure facilities are quite high, 2. Failure in the plan and policies of the consortium may spoil the entire system, 3. Demand for extra money by publishers for off consortia delivery of documents either in electronic or paper format, 4. Open access to shared resources is restricted and 5. Problems in online access due to server problems.

Library Digitization

It is the process of utilizing computers, databases, multimedia equipment, networks, video equipment and web technologies to electronically collect, classify, copy, compress, scan, store and transform conventional information sources. Library digitization is different from digital library as it focuses on the process of making diverse library information sources electronically available.

Library Management Software (LMS)

LMS has been developed to handle basic housekeeping functions of a library. It usually comprises a relational database, software to interact with that database and two geographical user interfaces i.e. one for administrator / staff and other for patrons. It has three basic functions to perform viz: Housekeeping operation, Public services and Administrative Planning or Decision-making.

An LMS is known as Integrated Library Management System (ILMS). The modules in ILMS include the following: *"1. Acquisition (ordering, receiving, accessioning, invoicing materials, etc.), 2. Cataloguing (Cataloging, indexing, materials, etc.), 3. Circulation (Patron management, issue materials to patrons, receiving them back, charge over dues, etc. 4. Serial Control (Ordering, receiving, tracking, magazine and newspaper holdings), 5. OPAC (Public Interface of users for search and retrieval), 6. Administration (administrative interface for the administration)"* (Gautam Kumar Sarma)

Library Network

It is a generic term and can mean several things to different people. Library Networks means libraries inter connected for the purpose of sharing of resources and techniques. These are essential to download bibliographic information for local cataloguing and to know about new publications and to share information resources.

A Library Network is formally defined as a set of inter-related information systems associated with communication facilities which adhere to more or less formal agreements and institutional arrangements, in order to jointly implement information handling operations with a view to pooling the resources and serving the users better.

Factors that effect the networking of libraries : 1. Willingness of the institutions / members to participate, 2. Agreement on standards and formats, 3. Creation of infrastructure for joining the network, 4. Compatibility of hardware and software, 5. Availability of communication technologies, and 6. Trained manpower.

Objectives : 1. To promote sharing of resources, 2. To offer guidance to member libraries on cataloguing, editing database services, circulation, acquisition, serial control, online services, relation of hardware and software, 3. To coordinate efforts for suitable collection development and reduce unnecessary duplication, 4. To establish referral center, 5. To facilitate and promote delivery of documents, 6. To develop special bibliographic database of books, serials and non-book materials, 7. To develop a database of projects, specialists and institutions, 8. To coordinate with other national and international networks for exchange of information and document, 9. To provide information to facilitate publication of newsletter or journals devoted to networking and sharing of resources.

Library Orientation

"The introduction of students and the faculty to the library, to location of essential areas and resources, basic elements of using the library and the services provided by libraries". (M. K. Goggin).

Library Portals

1. These are searchable, browsable and customizable presentation of library's valuable electronic resources. Information needs and was of library patrons can be well supported by library portals as they provide users with convenient, customized web-based access to a comprehensive collection of resources of relevance and authority.

2. These are sub-set of web portals which are organized gateways that help to structure access to information found the Internet (E. Miller).

Areas of coverage in the library portals: 1. Professional resources such as practical manuals, standards, reports and studies, 2. Organizations from large national associations to local and special interest groups, 3. Publications both print and electronic, 4. Conferences and other events, 5. Library websites, 6. Communication channels, 7. Job announcements, 8. Library market place i.e. vendors of library related products and services.

Benefit of Library Portals: 1. Easy access for users, 2. Simplified authentication, 3. Unified presentation of quality resources, 4. Personalization, groups of users can be offered clusters of resources, and 5. The portal may be a mechanism by which to offer services to an Institutional Portal.

Library Resource

It means "…. any and all materials, functions and services which constitute a modern library system. It is an amalgamation of people (manpower) processes, ideas, materials and money which form the substance of a library – can be described as its resources". (J. Fetterman).

Library Survey

It provides a frank evaluation of the services of a library by an outside agency so that library services can be streamlined / stimulated / strengthened. It is a systematic collection of data concerning libraries, their activities, operation, staff, use and users at a given time and period.

Library Technical Services

It can be defined as a mix of skilled and professional jobs to provide user services in libraries. Bibliographic control constitutes the essence of technical services. Cataloging and Classification in turn form inner core of bibliographic control processes.

Library Web Home Page

It serves as a promotional tool advertising in-house library services and electronic information resources on the Web. The pages should include an e-mail links to the library making the library easy to contact. Suitable information about the organization, collection, services and staff of the library, useful links to electronic resources etc., may be kept on the website.

Lifelong Learning

"A continuously supportive process that stimulates and empowers individuals to acquire all the knowledge, values, skills and understanding they will require throughout their life times and to apply them with confidence, creativity and enjoyment in all roles, circumstances and environments". (World Initiative on Lifelong Learning, 1994).

Limited Period Access Rights

This model is similar to renting or leasing the access rights for a limited period which could vary from one month to one year or more. Consumer models are available direct to end users where a user can license access rights on a monthly payment / usage model which of course will not be appropriate for libraries.

Linked In

It is a gateway to get posting and finding on jobs, sharing experience and answering questions. It is one of the best locations to connect with current and post coworkers and potentially future employers for professionals to get library patrons connected with the people that can help them find information.

Literature Review

"Literature review is a comprehensive survey of the works published in a field of study or related to a particular line of research usually in the form of a bibliographic essay or annotated list of references in which attention is drawn to the most significant works". (Anne's Encyclopedic Dictionary of Library and Information Science).

Living Archive

When describing an archive of specialty plants and individual who has an abundance of knowledge of various past events or reviving forgotten plays that capture social issues of their times is known as living archive.

Local History Collection

A collection of books, maps, prints, illustrations and other material relating a specific locality. Various types of documents: Books, Magazines, Memorial Volumes, Reports / Proceedings, Handbills / Leaflets, Newspaper Clippings, Maps, Posters, Charts, A. V. Material, Non-print documents and Personal Collection and Institutional Collections.

Logic Programming

It can be designed broadly as "the use of symbolic logic for explicit presentation of problems and their associated knowledge bases, together with the use of controlled logical inference for the effective of those problems. Logic programming is useful for stating problems and it is useful for representing the pragmatic information for effective problem solving" (R. Kowlaski and C. J. Hogger).

MALIBNET (Madras Library Network)

This was registered as a society in February 1993 and the Network became operational in June 1993.

Objectives : 1. To bring about cooperative working

amongst the libraries and information centers in the city of Madras (Chennai) in particular and in the State of Tamil Nadu in general, 2. To evolve a network of libraries and information centers in and around Madras region initially and in other parts of the State, 3. To facilitate sharing of resources among libraries and information centers, 4. To establish appropriate linkages with other regional, national and international libraries and information centers and 5. To organize conferences, workshops, seminars and arrange lectures in the field of internet.

MOOCs

MOOCs stand for Massive Open Online Courses. The term MOOC was derived in 2008 by Dave Cornier of the University of Prince Edward Island and Bryan Alexander of the National Institute for Technology in Liberal Education. MOOCs are of a very recent origin in distance education started somewhere around mid of 2011. It facilitates the availability of learning concepts to the large number of people, through the internet for global participation and also creates a prospect to learn at various levels of courses in colleges and universities to improve quality of education.

Advantages: 1. Save time, 2. Give best teachers access to more students, 3. Students learn at their own space, 4. On the first level, students can get immediate feedbacks on assignments, 5. No coaching charges, 6. Approach to top level professors in the organization to the external world, 7. Cooperation between Peers and Students, 8. Global Knowledge sharing among professors.

MYLIBNET (Mysore Library Network)

It was set up during May 1995 in the City of Mysore with the financial assistance of from NISSAT. It is housed in the premises of Central Food Technological Research Institute (CFTRI), Mysore.

Objectives: 1. To share resources available with all the libraries, 2. To provide faster communication to all the libraries through e-mail facility, 3. To develop software tools for better library management, 4. To create awareness in the field of latest information technology by conducting seminars / workshops / training programs, 5. To setup information base in collaboration with Industries and 6. To flash arrival of new books / journals, announcement of events like Seminars / Workshops / training programs.

Mainframe Computers

These are third generation computers introduced in 1960s. These range from small to very large. These are used to process a high volume batch application, to manage large databases and to act as central host computers in distributed systems and to perform thousands of other tasks. By virtue of large processing capacity, main frame computers can process data faster than mini computers and personal computers. In these computers several processors are used to process several tasks simultaneously at a time.

Maitrayee

This package has been developed by CMC, Calcutta (Kolkata) for Calcutta Libraries Network (CALIBNET) with the support of NISSAT, New Delhi. The package has been developed on INGRES as the underlying framework and works in UNIX environment. It is the first package which has been developed in India for a library network programme, providing specific network and communication facilities using TCP/IP as the communication software with X.25 protocol in addition to library management functions.

Maker Spaces

Places that help cultivate creative interests, imagination and passion by allowing participants to draw upon multiple intelligences. They are an effective means of applying knowledge and they tap new resources for learning. Maker spaces embrace tinkering or playing in various forms of exploration, experimentation and engagement and faster peer interactions as well as interests of collective team. (T. Wong).

Management Information System (MIS)

1. Kelly defined MIS as "a Combination of human and computer based resources that result in collection, storage, retrieval, communication and use of data for the purpose of efficient management of operations and for business planning".

2. According T. Lucy "a system to convert data from internal and external sources in to information and to communicate that information in an appropriate form to managers at all levels in all functions to enable them to make timely and effective decisions for planning, directing and controlling the activities for which they are responsible".

3. "A Management Information System (MIS) is the process and structure used by an organization to identify, collect, evaluate, transfer and utilize information in order to fulfill its objectives" (Peter Zorkoczy).

Characteristics : 1. Specific content of the information input, 2. Selectivity of the data, 3. Time lag, 4. Accuracy, 5. Reliability, 6. Generality and 7. Flexibility.

Manpower Planning

"Strategy for acquisition, utilization, improvement and retention of a enterprise's human resources" (Dept. of Employment, Govt. of India).

Need: 1. Ensures that an adequate supply of manpower is available, 2. Facilitate as a better understanding of behavioral pattern of employees, 3. Helps to prevent the need for suddenly dismissing employees, and 4. Aids for the provision of facilities which will be required by the employees.

Marketing

1. "Marketing is the process of planning and executing the concept of pricing, promotion, distribution of ideas, goods, services, organizations and event to create and maintain relationship that will satisfy individuals and organizational objectives". (D. L. Kurtz and L. E. Boone).
2. "Marketing is planning that focuses on products, place or mode of delivery, adjustment of cost / price to that market and promotion to specifically targeted segment of the special librarians' market" (Zachest and Williams).
3. "Marketing is the process of creating value through the creation of time, place and formalities" (Goldhar).

Marketing Concepts : 1. Market segmentation, 2. Consumer analysis, 3. Market positioning, 4. Marketing Program and 5. Market Audit (Zacharet and Williams)

Marketing in Libraries

Some of reasons for marketing in libraries could be: offer benefits to users want, reduce barriers to use and access, persuade and inform the user about the services library could offer and carefully plan to satisfy users need exceedingly. J. K. Cram opined that "Marketing is so basic that it cannot be considered a separate function within the library. Marketing is a central dimension of the entire library. It is entirely of the library's operations and services seen from a point of its final result, that is, from the customer's point of view".

Marketing Library Resources, Services and Products

M. Madhusudan identified the following reasons: 1. Providing solutions to dwindling budgets, 2. Promotion of products and services, 3. Help in gaining self-sufficiency, 4. Improves library image, 5. Create perception of information need in the library user, 6. Save from devaluation and providing sustainability to library profession, 7. Increase readership in the library, 8. User education, 9. Implication of five laws of library science, and 10. Solution for growing information.

Marketing Management (MM)

It is "the process of planning and executing the conception, pricing, promotion and distribution of ideas, goods and services to create exchanges that satisfy individual and organizational objectives" (American Marketing Association). Philip Kotler defined it as "Satisfying needs and wants through an exchange process". It aims at: *"1. Identification of the client base, 2. Determination of the needs, wants and demands of the client base and 3. Fulfillment of the same through designing and delivering appropriate products and/or services more effectively than competitors"* (RoshanRaina).

Mass Media

1. "A medium of communication (such as radio, television, newspaper, etc.) that reaches large number of people" (O.E.D.).
2. "Any of the means of communication such as television or newspaper that reaches very large number of people".
3. "The particular communication form used in presenting the written material, radio, TV, cable, cassette, film, live performance, holography, audio-recording or whatever medium or media are chosen" (A Dictionary of Media Terms).

Form of mass media : 1. Newspapers, Raidio, Cinema, T.V. and Video.

Functions : 1. Dissemination of information, 2. Socialization, 3. Motivation, 4. Education, 5. Cultural Promotion, 6.Entertainment and 7. Integration.

Medical Subject Headings (MeSH)

It is a thesaurus of over 19,000 main headings, 1,14,000 supplementary concept records and an entry of vocabulary of over 300,000 terms. MeSH is published of National Library of Medicine, USA. MeSH comprise National Library of Medicine (NLM's) controlled Vocabulary used for indexing articles, for cataloguing books and other holdings for searching MeSH indexed databases including MEDLINE. MeSH terminology provides consistent way for retrieval information that may use different terminology for the same concepts.

Marketing mix

It means the variables on which the organization has control and are used in different combinations / mixes to satisfy the target market. A typical marketing mix consists of product or service offerings at a price, targeting a customer segment in certain place and a set of modalities to reach the target customer and promotion to tell the potential customers about the availability of the offering.

Elements of marketing mix : 1. Product planning, 2. Branding, 3. Packing, 4. Servicing, 5. Channels of distribution, 6. Physical handling, 7. Pricing, 8. Advertising, 9. Promotions, 10. Display, 11. Personal selling, 12. Fact finding and analysis.

Marketing Research

It provides systematic design, collection, analysis, reporting of data relevant to specific marketing situation facing an organization. It is a vehicle by which information is obtained about present and prospective marketing mixes, the changing character of the external environment and the degree to which existing marketing programme are achieving their goals and is essential in university libraries.

Marketing via Website

Website of a library is a vital tool to share the vision and mission. It is a handy tool to announce the yearly plan, new additions and new initiatives of the library. The resources acquired by the library can be delivered to users in a systematic way by building a website of the library.

Matter (Attribute or Property) [M]

The fundamental cater Matter [M] manifest isolate ideas or concepts representing intrinsic matter, material, properties, attributes of entity / object or entity / object set that is qualities, quantities, etc. For example: Printed book. In the Main Class (MC) printed book comes under Matter Facet.

Media

It refers to various means of mass communication, thought of as a whole, including television, radio, magazines and newspapers together with the people involved in their production.

Media and Information Literacy

"Media and Information Literacy is a set of competencies that empowers citizens to access, retrieve, understand, evaluate and use, create as well as share information and media content in all formats, using various tools in a critical, ethical and effective way in order to participate and engage in personal, professional and social activities" (UNESCO).

Media Library

This supports professional activities of journalists. It acquires preserves and makes available of archival and special collection materials of national and regional significance relating audio-visual and media communities and popular culture. This includes film / video production, advertising, electronic and print journalism broadcasting, photographic arts, multi-media and music production. These collections are contained in the form of audio, video, photographic, digital and print media formats.

Medical Informatics

Blois and Shortliffe defined it as "a storage, retrieval and optimal use of biomedical information, data and knowledge for problem solving and decision making".

Melvin Voigt's Users' Approach

Melvin Voigt a great exponent of users approach to seek information as far back as in 1961 identified three approaches by which users seek information.

Approach to information	Category of information sources
Current Approach	Primary Information
Everyday Approach	Secondary Information
Exhaustive Approach	Secondary / Tertiary Information

Meta Archive

This was began in 2004 as a venture led by Emory University with Georgia Technical University, University of Louis Villa, Virginia Technological University, Auburn University, Florida State University and Library of Congress.

Metadata

1. It is the descriptive and classification of information about digital object or digital resource such as web page, a computer file, an image, multimedia document, etc. It gives complete description about a digital object and is crucial for preserving and sharing such resources.
2. It may be defined as representing a higher level of information that describes the content, context, quality, structure and accessibility of a specific data set such as digital data images, databases and printed materials.

Need of Metadata : 1. Resource identification and location, 2. Resource documentation, 3. Resource selection, evaluation and assessment, 3. Improving quality and quantity of search results, 4. Content reuse, 5. Efficient content development and archiving, 6. Protecting intellectual property rights, and 7. Electronic commerce to encode prices, terms of pay, etc.

Types of Metadata: 1. Administrative, 2. Descriptive, 3. Preservation, 4. Technical, 5. Use.

Metadata Harvesting Protocols

It is a set of rules for harvesting metadata from different sources. Specified set of protocols guides and helps to harvest metadata to start service to search it at a single place and guide the users to access the full-text from individual repository. The major need of metadata harvesting protocol is to finding means to discover easily the already existing electronic contents.

Meta Search Engine

"Meta search engine, also known as Metacrawler or multi-threaded engine is a search tool that allow searches to be sent to several search engines,, web directories and sometimes to the so called invisible (Deep) Web all at once. Unlike search engines, meta search engines don't crawl the web themselves to build databases. Instead, the results are blended together in one page. They are also referred to as parallel search engines, multithreaded search engines or mega search engines". (Daniel Bazac).

Micro CAIRS (Micro Computer Assisted Information Retrieval System)

It is a flexible, low cost microcomputer base Information Retrieval software System. The programmes have been written in RTL2, a high level computer language, which allows MCAIRS to run on most popular microcomputers. It was designed by professional information scientists at the Leatherhead Food Research Association, U.K. for library information management requirements.

Microcomputers

There are smallest units and tiny special purposes devices dedicated to a single task such as time keeping in wrist watches or controlling an automobile ignition system. These are very familiar personal computers ranging from desktop to pocket size that we can use in a number of ways. These can perform the same operations and use the same type of instructions as much larger computers. These give people personal processing capabilities.

Microform

It is an important medium of information storage. It includes all carriers of information in the form of microfilm or similar optical media containing micro images too small to be read without magnification. Micrographics refer to the technology or system associated with the production, handling and use of microforms.

Characteristics: 1. Type of information (size and layout), 2. Density of information, 3. Polarity of micro-images, 4. Optical transfer properties of micro images.

Advantages or reasons for the use of microforms: 1. Space saving, 2. Security of documentation, 3. Economy of filing, 4. Economy and ease of copying, 5. Economy of distribution, 6. Organizational advantage, 7. Economy of file up-to-date, 8. Retrieval speed, and 9. Speed and Economy of recording.

Disadvantages : 1 Costly equipment, 2. High costs of maintenance and preservation, 3. No provision for marginal notes, 4. Poor equipment and poor recording causes health hazards i.e. eye strain, stiff neck trouble, etc.

Micrographics

It is a technique of using opaque or transparent media as a carrier of miniature raised permanent message, e.g. Microfilm, microfiche, etc. The development in photographic emulsions with very high resolution is the main factor in producing unbelievably small images on the carrier, leading to the production of ultra fiche. Other useful formats are: Ultra fiche, micro-opaque, aperture cards, computer output microfiche / microfilm and jacket.

Microsoft Windows Azure

Windows Azure is a cloud platform of Microsoft Corporation that empowers organizations to develop and run applications with unbounded scalability and ease-of-use. With this flexible platform one can easily scale up or down to meet the demands of business.

Micro text

It is text with explicit links among its components. A micro text system provides computer medium for manipulating the links of micro text. A micro text system supports browsing. The first micro text was called Augmentation System and was developed in the 1960s as an authoring and browsing tool.

Migration

It means of overcoming technological obsolescence by transferring digital data resources from one hardware / software generation to next. The purpose of migration is to preserve the intellectual content of digital objects and to retain the ability for clients to retrieve, display and other wise use them in the face of constantly changing technology.

Mini Computers

These are small general purpose systems but they serve multiple users. These are more powerful than micros and less powerful than main frames. In size these vary from desktop models to the size of small file cabinets. Minis are used for single specialized applications or a number of general applications in small organizations. These can be used for high speed transactions in a financial companies and industries.

Mobile Collections

These span a wide range content and equally wide range of delivery methods. These include access to reference sources to audio-book collections and databases (L. Murray).

Mobile Device

It is a portable, wireless computing device that is small enough to be used while held in the hand. The mobile devices are reshaping lives of every citizen in diverse ways, especially by delivering content in versatile forms.

Mobile Learning

The use of portable devices equipped with Internet facility in the learning process. M-Learning facilitates oneself to learn, collaborate, and share their ideas with each other in short time using Internet technology.

Mobile Library Websites

An important component of a mobile library services. It is basically a short version of large website that is designed and optimized for viewing on mobile services. They may be even hosted on their own sub-domain. The general purpose of a mobile website is to make the content or at least a subset of the content available to users. Mobile websites complement the existing library websites and help extend resources and information to users through their mobile devices.

Mobile Commerce

It refers to retail marketing via mobile devices, allowing retailers and consumers to trade and interact on wireless networks using smart phones, I-Pads and Tablets. Services include online purchases, promotion, mobile advertising, relationship building activities and customer support. It is a platform which enables users to do any sort of transactions like buying and selling of goods asking any services, transferring the ownership or rights', transacting and transferring the money accessing wireless internet service on the mobile handset itself.

Mobile Reading

It is the act of reading and consuming digital content on mobile services such as phones, tablets, PCs, e-readers and which covers e-books, e-newspapers, e-magazines and mobile cartoons. The rapid development of mobile reading promoted the mobile publishing industry.

Advantages : a) Portability, b) Capacity, c) Better readings, d) Avoiding Annoyances, e) Free books and f) gain of space.

Mobile Technology

It is the technology used for Cellular Communication Multiple Code Division Multiple Access (CDMA) Technology evolved rapidly over the past few years. It is portable, it refers to any device that one can carry with him to perform wide variety of tasks. Mobile technology in the form of phones, tablet and notebooks is making our lives better than ever before.

Devices : 1. Laptop and computers, 2. Mobile Phones, 2. GPS-enabled devices, 4. Wireless smart card payment terminals.

Motivation

It is a managerial process that encourages an employee to fulfill the organizational goals. The needs of an employee will be identified and tries to satisfy them to make a job alternative. Motivated employee find better ways to perform the job, to improve quality of work and tries for better results.

Multimedia (MM)

1. It means the integration of various individual media such as texts, graphics, animation, video-clips and sound

files into a digital environment. It has the ability to represent the data in an interactive and attractive environment through user friendly interfaces and hypertext links.
2. It is the convergence of computers and communication technology and is a system which integrates text, voice and voice-processing, film pictures, etc. MM lets out use several types of media like sound, graphics, animation, texts etc.

Components : 1. Text, 2. Graphics, 3. Animations, 4. Sound, 5. Image, 6. Speech, 7. Score, 8. Movie, 9. Object, 10. World.

Constituents of MM : 1. Computer with processor and RAM, 2. Display Unit (TV or Monitor), 3. Means of user interactive device, 3. Hard disc with at least 120 MB, 4. CD-Drive, 5. Sound Systems, 6. Headphone.

Multimedia Instructional System

It refers to the uses of appropriate and carefully selected varieties of learning experiences which are presented to the learner through select teaching strategies. Multimedia includes: Overhead Projector, slides, transparences in the motion pictures video cassettes, Television, CD-ROMs, Laser Discs, Digital Audio Tape, like Maps, charts, illustrations, graphic materials, flow diagrams, plans, graphs, photographic enlargements, cartoons, magnetic tape disk recordings, cartoons, etc. Silent and sound film strips, digital audio tape, like maps, charts, illustrations, graphic materials, flow diagrams, planes graphics, photographic enlargements, cartoons, magnetic tape disk recordings, cartoons, etc.

Characteristic of multimedia system : 1. Contain more information and have many terminals through which students (learners) have access to the information, 2. Offer students many ways to learn to large number of things, 3. Large number of learning models can be offered, 4. Permits delivery of a range of instructional and informational support, 5. Capability is greater than that of ordinary class room practice.

Advantages : 1. Provides teacher with more sources of information for effective teaching, 2. Assists the teacher in overcoming the physical difficulties of presentation of a concept subject or theme, 3. Provides professional and job satisfaction to the teaching community.

Multimedia Information

Multimedia information results from the integration of data, text, images and sound within a single electronic information environment.

Multiple Authorship

The synonymous terms used to refer to 'multiple authorship' are: joint authorship, mixed authorship, co-authorship, etc. According to S. R. Ranganathan joint authorship means "two or more authors sharing responsibility for the thought and expression constituting the work, the portion for which each is separately responsible not being specified or separable". According to AACR-II "a person who collaborates with the one or more other person to produce a work in relation to which the collaborators perform the same function".

Museum

"A Museum is an organized and permanent non-profit institution essentially educational or aesthetic in purpose with professional staff, which owns and utilities tangible objects, cares for them and exhibit them to the public on some regular schedule" (American Association of Museums). Modern museums of any kind, acquire, conserve, research and communicate the value and significance of materials relating to history, culture and civilization of a country.

Museum Library

A library attached to a museum and must posses a well equipped staff and useful collections and play very important role in promoting study and research, disseminating knowledge, fostering learning and promoting education.

Main Objectives : 1. To buildup useful collection of books and other reading materials, 2. To act as an active study and research centre and to promote quality research, 3. To aid and support researchers by proving required information, 4. To compile bibliographies and offer documentation and reference services, 5. To strive for interlibrary cooperation, 6. To provide necessary forum for self-study and research by the curatorial staff and to keep abreast of latest developments in its special field.

Music Library

It may be distinct entity or department of a larger library. It concentrates on musical materials i.e. books, scores and recordings exist in various formats. May have books in electronic form, scores on microfilm or paper and recordings on disc, tape or in any digital form. Music Libraries may also have holdings of a museum character such as actual instruments and items associated with the composers, performers and other personalities associated with music world.

N

NASSDOC (National Social Sciences Documentation Centre)

It is a division of Indian Council of Social Science Research (ICSSR) and is responsible for information support service to social scientists. Major programmes of NASSDOC includes: 1. Library and Reference Service, 2. Literature search and bibliography on demand service, 3. Preparation of Abstracts and indexes, of major Indian Social Science Periodicals, 4. Compilation of 'an events calendar' incorporating details of forthcoming conferences / seminars, etc., 4. Document delivery service, and 5. Financial assistance to research scholars for visiting libraries / archives to collect research material.

NETTLIB

M/s Kaptson Pvt. Ltd, produced this software. This was an integrated Library Management Software with capability to work on network or standalone configuration. This software was developed on Visual Basic 6.0 and works in conjunction with RDBMS (Relational Database Management System) like SQL / ORACLE / SYBASE, etc. Its cost was Rs. 50,000/- in addition to the cost of the SQL server which costs Rs. 50,000/. This software can be accessed from other networks through Web Interface or dedicated lines (LAN / WAN) compatible. It can convert data from one format to any other and vice-versa. Publicity literature indicates that (1) this is the first Library Management Software to support Indian language and undertakes retro-conversion job both onsite, as well as at its own premises.

NICNET (National Informatics Centre Network)

National Informatics Centre (NIC) is premier S&T organization, Govt. of India in the field of Informatics services and I.T. applications. It has been instrumental in the application of IT in the Government Departments at the Centre, States and District facilitating improvement in government services, wider transparency in government functions and improvement in decentralized planning and management. To facilitate this NIC has established a nationwide ICT Network called NICNET – with gateway nodes at about 53 Central Government Departments, 35 State / UTI Secretariats and 603 District Collectorates for IT Services. *See also National Informatics Centre (NIC).*

NISSAT Newsletter

In cooperation with the Society for Information Science (SIS), NISSAT has been publishing its quarterly *NISSAT Newsletter*. It covers wide range of issues relating to information and the development of information services networks and centres. Individuals and professional bodies are invited to contribute features and news items on new concepts and services, seminars, training courses, new products, status of information both national and international trends in their development.

NISTADS (National Institute of Science, Technology and Development Studies)

The Council of Scientific and Industrial Research (CSIR) realizing the need for well thought out science policy input into the national planning process constituted in 1974 the Centre for the Study of Science, Technology and Development (CSSTD). This Centre was subsequently given the status of an autonomous institute of CSIR and renamed as NISTADS in 1981. In 1982, the Centre for Management Development (CMD), which was till then working as part of CSIR Headquarters, was also merged with NISTADS.

Objectives : 1. To carry out research in the areas of Science, Technology and Society, 2. To provide consultancy services and undertake sponsored research, 3. To provide training to scholars and functionaries from India and abroad, 4. To undertake cooperative research projects and provide research opportunities to scholars through various schemes and 5. To disseminate information in its areas of specialization.

N-LIST (National Library and Information Services Infrastructure for Scholarly Contents

This Project jointly executed by the UGC-INFONET Digital Library Consortium, INFLIBNET Centre and INDEST-AICTE, IIT (Delhi) for (i) Cross subscription to E-resources subscribed by the two consortia i.e. subscription to INDESI-AICTE resources for Universities and UGC-INFONET resources for technical institutions and(ii) Access to selected e-resources to Government / Government aided colleges. This project provides more than 3000 + e-journals and 75,000 + e-books to students, researchers and faculty members from colleges covered under section 123 of UGC Act.

NPTEL

It is a programme on Technology Enhanced Learning which was initiated by seven Indian Institutes of Technology (IITs-Bombay, Delhi, Guwahati, Kanpur, Kharagpur, Madras and Roorkee) and Indian Institute of Bangalore for creating course contents in engineering and science. It was originated from many deliberations between IITs, IIMs and Carnegie Mellon University (USA) during the years 1999-2003. A proposal for creating contents for 100 courses as web based supplements and 100 complete video courses for 40 hours duration per course was mooted.

NTIS (National Technical Information Service), USA

NTIS provides access to information on US Government sponsored research and development projects. US Government sponsored research is conducted through three major agencies viz. Department of Energy (DoE), Department of Defense (DoD) and National Aeronautical and Space Administration (NASA). Research conducted by these agencies result in technical reports which are made available through NTIS clearing house. NTIS classifies the reports under COSATI (Committee on Science and Technology) categories under each there is a sub-classification. Reports are accessioned in NTIS collection and each report will have two report numbers – one is the NTIS accession number and the other is the original report number. NTIS also receives reports from a number of other agencies.

NTIS Data Base

NTIS created a database for all the reports published since 1964. It is regularly updated by including in its collection all the reports that are accessioned by NTIS. It also publishes a fortnightly journal *Government Reports & Announcement Index* (GRAI). This is an abstracting journal containing information on US Government reports received at NTIS headquarters.

National Assessment and Accreditation Council (NAAC) of UGC

UGC has established an autonomous body called NAAC to assess and accredit institutions of higher education and learning in the Country. It is the outcome of the recommendations of *National Policy of Education* (1986) that laid emphasis on achieving quality in higher education in India. It was established in 1994 with is headquarters at Bangalore. It (NAAC) functions through its General Council (GC) and Executive Committee (EC) where educational administrators, policy makers and senior academicians are represented. The Chairperson of the UGC is President of the GC of the NAAC, the Chair Person of the EC is an eminent academician in the area of relevance to the NAAC. The Director of NAAC is its academic and administrative Head and is the Member-Secretary of both GC and EC.

National Bibliographic Centre (NBC)

The National Bibliographic Centre in the Indian context is as follows: 1. *To prepare current national bibliography and to develop automated system for publication of the Indian National Bibliography (INB), 2. To prepare retrospective bibliography, 3. To prepare national union catalogue of major libraries, 4. To prepare general bibliographies and special bibliographies, 5. To promote library cooperation for bibliographic activities, 6. To render bibliographic information services, 7. To undertake and sponsor bibliographic research, 8. To adopt and promote adoption of international bibliographic standards and 9. To exchange* bibliographic research with other countries by agreements, 10. To participate in international bibliographic projects and systems, 11. To coordinate bibliographic activities of different institutions, organizations and individuals, 12. To function as a central bibliographic referral center, 13. To undertake user education programs, and 14. To undertake any other activity conducive to the promotion of bibliographic services in the country.

National Book Trust (NBT), India

It started functioning since 1957 as an autonomous body under the Ministry of Education, (now Ministry of Human Resources Development), Government of India. A small cabinet-like committee manages the affairs of the Trust.

Main Objectives : 1. To produce good literature in Engish as well as regional languages and to inculcate reading habits among children, 2. To faster book-mindedness in the country by providing best works from one language into another.

It is also supposed to take care of:1. Translation of works from one regional language into another, and 2. Children's literature.

National Digital Infrastructure and Preservation Programme (NDIPP)

This programme of Library of Congress (LC) aims at collecting, preserving and making available significant digital content for current and future generations. LC through this programme has collaborated with various libraries and organizations for preserving at risk digital content in to over 1400 collections and built a distributed digital preservation infrastructure.

National Digital Library of India (NDL-India)

A pilot project under National Mission on Education with the aid of Information and Communication Technology (ICT) was initiated at IIT Kharagpur to develop framework of virtual search facility. Filtered and federated searching is employed to facilitate focused searching so that learners can find out the right resource with least effort and in minimum time. It is being developed to help students to prepare for entrance and competitive examinations, to enable people to learn and prepare from best practices from all over the world and to facilitate researchers to perform interlinked exploration from multiple sources.

National Informatics Centre (NIC)

NIC of the Department of Information Technology Government of India has been providing network backbone and e-governance support Central Government, State Governments, UT Administrations, Districts and other Government bodies. NIC offers a wide range of ICT services including Nationwide Communication Network for decentralized planning, improvement in Government services and wider transparency of national and local governments. NIC assists in implementing IT Projects in close collaboration with Central and State Governments in areas such as: 1. Centrally sponsored schemes and Central Sector Schemes, 2. State sector and State sponsored projects and 3. District Administration sponsored projects. It endeavors to ensure that latest technology in all spheres of IT is available to its clientele.

Services : 1. Software design and development, 2. Networking, 3. Internet services, 4. WWW Services, 5. Video Conferencing, 6. Multimedia, 7. Geographical Information System (GIS), 8. E-Commerce, 9. Rural Informatics, 10. Training, 11. Bibliographic Informatics, 12. Patent Information, etc.

National Information Policy

A set of decisions taken by a government through the appropriate laws and regulations, to orient the harmonious development of the information transfer activities in order to satisfy the information needs of the country. A National Policy needs the provision of concrete implementation means i.e. financial, personnel and institutional.

Goals: 1. To ensure optimum utilization of accumulated knowledge, 2. To ensure availability of adequate information for making decisions in all spheres of national activity, 3. To provide information services relevant to the present needs, 4. To focus attention of the governments and private organizations on the problem of information availability and 5. To promote national and international cooperation on the exchange of information and expertise.

National Information System

1. A set of discipline mission or function oriented information systems i.e. the information infrastructure, operating in a coordinated way and through the use of specified techniques of information handling in accordance with the goals established by the national information policy in order to satisfy the needs of the users at large.

2. It is basically a network of existing information resources together with new services for identified gaps, so coordinated as to reinforce and enhance the activities of individual units and thus enable specific categories of users to receive the information relevant to their needs and abilities (P. Atherton).

3. "A national information system can be envisaged as a total information network in the few central bodies at the apex for coordination, a number of sectorial centers, national in scope but discipline / product / mission oriented and a number of local information units, operating to meet the immediate requirements of a particular organization. These are integrative organic parts of the system, operating independently without any administrative red tape from any single top organization" (T. N. Rajan).

National Institute of Science Communication (NISCOM)

This Institution had been in existence for the last six decades (first as two publication units of CSIR, which were merged to form the Publication Division, which was later renamed as Publications & Information Directorate and in 1996 as NISCOM). Over the years, NISCOM diversified its activities and through a host of its information products comprising research and popular science journals, encyclopedic publications, monographs, books and information services, it had been reaching out to researchers, students, entrepreneurs, industrialists, agriculturists, policy planners and also the common man. This was merged in NISCAIR in the year 2002.

National Institute of Science Communication and Information Resources (NISCAIR)

It came into existence on September 30, 2002 consequence to the merger of National Institute of Science Communication (NISCOM) and Indian National Scientific Documentation Centre (INSDOC). Both NISCOM and INSDOC, the two prestigious institutions of CSIR were earlier devoted dissemination and Documentation of Scientific and Technical Information.

Now with the formation of NISCAIR all the activities of NISCOM and INSDOC have been amalgamated making NISCAIR an institute capable of serving the scientific community using modern IT infrastructure in a more effective and efficient manner and taking up new ventures in the field of science communication, dissemination and S&T information management systems and services. Broadly the core activity of NISCAIR is to collect, store, publish and disseminate S&T information through a mix of traditional and modern means which will benefit different segments of scientific community. The Institute offers a course called Associate ship in Information Science (AIS).

The National Knowledge Commission (NKC) (India)

The National Knowledge Commission, India was setup in the year 2005, by the Government of India, as a high level Advisory Body to the Prime Minister of India, with a mandate to guide policy and generate reforms. The Commission said to be the world's first body of its kind. It prime focus was on five key areas such as: access to knowledge, knowledge concepts, knowledge creation, knowledge application and development of better knowledge services. Dr. Sam Pitroda was appointed as Chairman of the Commission. In respect of libraries, the Commission had set up a Working Group on Libraries to initiate object review of current services and standards and to recommend the changes India needs.

Objectives : 1. Creation of Knowledge principally depends on strengthening education system, promoting domestic research and innovation in laboratories as well as at the grass root level, 2. Application of Knowledge will primarily target the sectors such as health, agriculture, government and industry. This involves diverse priorities like using traditional knowledge in agriculture, encouraging innovation in industry and agriculture, 3. Dissemination of Knowledge focuses on ensuring universal element any education, specially for girls and using information and communication technology (ICT) to enhance standards in education and widely disseminate easily accessible knowledge that is useful to public.

National Knowledge Network (NKN)

It is a high speed nationwide network by Government of India, with a high bandwidth of 1 gb ps. Its implementing agency is National Informatics Centre (NIC). There is provision in NKN to attend video-conferencing and e-learning classes from distant virtual classrooms.

National Library (India), Kolkata

The National Library in India has a very rich heritage and

the basic collection goes back to Calcutta Public Library which was established in 1836. The same collection was merged with the then Imperial Library and it was formally opened for the public in 1903. The library became the National Library by an Act of Parliament in 1948. The main functions of the National Library as a bibliographic Centre have been laid down in the recommendations of the Review Committee (1969) and the High-powered Committee on National Policy on Library and Information System of 1986. According to these recommendations, the National Library is expected to act as follows:

1. Rendering of bibliographical and documentation services on retrospective material, both general and specialized, 2. Acting as a referral center purveying full and accurate knowledge of all sources of bibliographic information and participation in international bibliographical activities, 3. Provision of photo-copying and reprographic services, 4. Acting as the Centre for International Book Exchange and International Loan, 5. To render to the nation and to the world bibliographical and other services to meet the requirements of different user groups, 6. To interface between the national systems and international systems wherever possible, and 7. To pay a role of leadership in the country in the task of expanding and improving the library and information services.

National Mission on Libraries (NML)

The National Mission on Libraries has been setup in 2009 and was launched in 2014 on the recommendations of National Knowledge Commission (NKC) which was setup by Government of India. One of the works assigned to the mission was to prepare National Census of all Libraries. In addition, it would design an adequate proforma and distribute them electronically and collect them in the same manner. The three important tasks set before mission was: 1. Census of all libraries in India, 2. Establishing Council for Library and Information Science, and 3. Building the National Public Library System with National Library of India.

National Mission for Manuscripts

It was set up by the Department of Culture, Government of India in 2009 seeks to develop holistic approach in locating, documenting, protecting and making accessible the significant information of the manuscripts heritage of India. Some of the objectives of the Mission are to survey, document, preserve and disseminate the existing Indian manuscripts. This challenging task will be carried out through wide networking with Institutions and scholars across the country and abroad who have manuscript holding and who have an active interest in their preservation. It has located more than a thousand partner institutions in the country with manuscript collections. It works with the help of 57MSS Resource Centres across the Country. These include well established institutes, museums, libraries, universities and non-governmental organizations that act as the Mission's coordinating agency in the respective regions.

National Mission on Education through Information and Communication Technology (NMEICT)

This mission was launched on 3rd February 2009. It initiated a project called "National Library and Information Service Infrastructure for Scholarly Content known as N-LIST. The N-List project is being jointly executed by the UGC-Information Network (UGC-INFONET), Digital Library Consortium, INFLIBNET Centre and the INDEST-AICTE Consortium, Indian Institute of Technology (IIT), Delhi The project provides access to selected resources to colleges through subscription to INDEST-AICTE resources and UGC-INFONET-Resources.

National Programme on Technology Enhanced Learning (NPTEL)

It was an initiative taken by seven Indian Institutes of Technology (Bombay, Delhi, Guwahati, Kanpur, Kharagpur, Madras and Roorkee) and Indian Institute of Science (IISc) for creating Course Consents in engineering and science. NPTEL as a project originated from many deliberations between IITs, Indian Institute of Management (IIMs) and Carnegie Mellon University (CMU) during 1990-2003.

National Repository of Open Educational Resources (NROER)

It is an initiative of Ministry of Human Resource Development (MHRD), Government of India and CIET-NCERT to bring together all digital and digitisable resources across all stages of school education and teacher education. This spans to all subject domain and will be available in all Indian languages. It proposes to use the digital resources to reach out and connect all members of the school community through a variety of events and interactions. The repository will also provide platform for Massive Open Online courses (MOOCs) and online forums for different stake holders.

Networking

Two or more computers connected together form a network to exchange data, share software and hardware resources. The server stores and manages programs and data, whereas the clients or nodes are the computers, from which users access data and programs stored in the server. In a local area network (LAN), the network is spread within a physical campus, whereas wide area network (WAN) span larger areas, like between cities or countries. The largest type of WAN is the Internet and the World Wide Web (WWW) is a system of information accessed through Internet. Telephone dialup line, lease line, radio, modem and VSAT are the most popular WAN connectivity media used currently to connect different computers and networks.

Components in a network: 1. Information resources, 2. Readers or users, 3. Schemes for organization of documents or data, 4. Methods for the delivery of resources to readers / users – the output, 5. Formal Organization and 6. Bidirectional communication networks.

Network Topology

A network system comprises of nodes and links. Network topology is the physical layout as well as connectivity among all the nodes in a network. Node can be called as the starting point or end point in this connectivity and it may be a terminal, computer, server, and work station, modem, etc.

The most basic network topologies are: *1. Star topology, 2. Bus topology, 3. Ring topology, 4. Tree topology, 5. Loop topology and 6. Mesh topology.*

Neural Network

1. "A neural network is made up of a number of processing elements called neuron, whose inter-connections are called synapses. Each neuron accepts inputs from either the external world or from the outputs of other neurons. Output signals from all neurons eventually propagate their effect across the entire network to the final layer where the results can be output to the real world". (D. J. Sarma and S. G. Sarma).

2. "A neural network is a system composed of many simple processing elements operating in parallel whose function is determined by network structure, connection strengths and processing performed computing elements or node" (S. Jojodia and B. Kogan).

New Gen Lib

New Gen Lib is an integrated library management system developed by Verus Solutions Pvt. Ltd. Domain expertise is provided by Kesavan Institute of Information and Knowledge Management, Hyderabad. New Gen Lib Version 1.0 was released in March 2005. In January 2008 a decision was taken to offer the system as OSS under the GNU GPL License by Verus Solutions. New Gen Lib complies with international metadata and inter-operability standards: *MARC-21, MARCX-XML, Z39.50, SRU/W, and OAI-PMH.*

Non-Book Materials

Publications other than printed books or conventional documents are called non-book materials. These by virtue of their nature, scope, purpose and structure require special treatment over books and periodicals. "Those library materials which do not come within the definition of a book, periodical or pamphlet and which require special handling e.g., A/V material, microforms, etc." (Harrod's Librarians Glossary).

Non-Conventional Media (NCM)

It covers the whole range of documents such as microforms (microfiche, aperture cards, magnetic storage and optical storage media, microfilm, etc.); audio (sound tape, disc etc.); visual (art reproductions, charts, photographic prints, slides, transparencies, film strips, etc.); audio-visual (cine film video cassettes, etc.). Non-book material and non-print material / media are the phrases used synonymously with NCM.

O

OCLC (Online Computer Library Centre)

It is a non-profit organization established in Ohio (USA) in 1967. It was founded by small group of libraries whose leaders believed by working together, they could find practical solutions for sharing records and reducing information costs.

Its aim was to use newly available computer technology to automate the traditional library catalogue. It rapidly became collaborative revolution, now involves thousands of libraries worldwide. It helps libraries to serve millions of users of academic, public, school and special libraries in 96 countries. More than 53,000 libraries all over the world use OCLC services to locate, acquire, catalogue, lend and preserve library materials.

OCLC Webscale

It has set an example for making use of cloud computing for libraries. For long years OCLC has been functioning as a cloud computing vendor because they provide cataloguing tools over the internet and allow member institutions to draw on their centralized data store (Robert Fox).

OPAC

An Online Public Access Catalogue is an online database of a library or group of Libraries holdings. Users can search to locate document and other reading material available at a library by different approaches like title, author, subject, etc. OPACs are the gateways to inform in libraries and provide facilities to browse search and locate information. OPACs were developed to meet the user community needs in two ways viz., 1. It meant access to library housekeeping operations especial circulation and 2. To give the library users direct access to the machine-readable bibliographic records.

OSS Labs

This OSS Labs from India is using Amazon's elastic cloud computing platform owing to various capabilities of Amazon such as high durability of data, strong information security based on ISO standards, scalability and flexibility. It is expected that OSS Labs will be able to provide robust based solutions to demanding customers.

Obsolescence

The use of information of a specific discipline or a document reaches a most when an exact period of your time right from its date of publication and thenceforth, it use gradually declines. This sort of relationship is usually expressed by the term obsolescence.

Occupational Stress

It means "negative environmental factors or stress (e.g.: work overload, role conflict / ambiguity, poor working condition) associated with a particular job" (Cooper and Marshall).

Ohio Link

It is a consortium of 88 colleges and Universities and the State Library of Ohio. Ohio Link's e-services include a multi publisher E-Journals Publisher Centre which was launched in 1998 provides access to more than 7000 scholarly journal titles from 40+ publishers across different disciplines. Ohio Link has declared its intension to maintain the EJC content as a permanent archive and has got perpetual archival rights in its license agreement.

Online Catalogue

It is essentially a computer based replacement of the old card catalogue and its purpose and functions remain the same. The online catalogue is a value added system which supersedes the functions of traditional card catalogue. It is beyond the capabilities of card catalogue to provide keyword search, Boolean searching and to provide interactive instructions or search facilities to users with possibility of getting outputs in various formats and information contents they require.

Advantages : The following are some of the important advantages: *1. Huge capacity to store enormous data, 2. Compact and saves lot of space in the library, 3. Can be used as interactive* multimedia and hyper media, 4. Can be updated very quickly, 5. Bibliographic data is fed only once, 6. Affords large and multiple approach searching capabilities, 7. Can be easily interfaced with documents acquisition and circulation system, and 8. Have integrated authority control system with cross-references.

Online Citation Tools

Some of the popular online citation tools are: 1. Bib Me, 2. Citation Wizard, 3. Citation Machine, 4. Easy Bib, 5. Knight Cite, 6. Mendeley, 7. Noodle tools, 8. RefWorks, 9. Zotero and 10. Otto Bib.

Online database/s

It is a database accessible from a network including from the internet. It differs from local database held in an individual computer or its attached storage such as CD.

The databases which are available in online are called 'online databases'. A database management is set of programmes that enable storing, modifying and extracting information from a database. Database servers hold actual data and run on the DBMS and related software.

Online Electronic Library

1. A system of distribution of full text and multimedia databases accessible on computer networks. It has a number of machine-readable publications and facilities for remote access to several databases.

2. The digital libraries as organizations that provide the resources, including specialized staff to select, offer intellectual access, to interpret, distribute, preserve the integrity of and ensure the persistence over time of collections of digital works so that they are readily and economically available for use by a defined community of set of communities". (The Digital Library Federation).

Objectives: 1. To collect, store, organize and disseminate information in digital form, 2. To save the time of the user as well as the library staff, 3. To provide accurate and right information at the right time, 4. To save space, 5. To provide information to a large number of user community at a time, 6. To reduce human effort and cost involved in different library activities and 7. To preserve valuable and rare documents.

Online Information Services

These services involve the services from remotely located databases through interactive communication with the help of computers and communication channels. The users can access the databases directly via a vendor (Supplier of online services). Generally online information services are those services which are available through networks.

Components : 1. Database producer or information provider, 2. Online service providers, 3. Tele communication links, 4. Workstation, and 5. Link tools.

Online exhibition

It is an event which can be viewed right on their home computers / mobiles using the Internet / General Packet Radio Service (GPRS) anywhere, any place any time. It is a way of disseminating information in digital form including exhibiting products, artifacts, educating visitors on any topic to an international audience throughout the year. The information will be delivered through web over the Internet and helps in doing e-commerce over Internet.

Benefits : 1. Enhanced learning by providing detailed information on exhibits, 2. Broadens access to the content, 3. Visitors to the exhibits are not limited to a particular location, 4. Serve as free resource for teachers for educational programmes, 5. Multimedia and virtual reality tools provide best interactivity.

Online Journal

"An online journal is a publication, often scholarly, that

is made accessible in a computerized format and distributed over Internet" (Amjad Ali).

Online Legal Information System (OLIS)

It is developed to suit Indian needs. It perpetrates numerous types of legal information resources in a single window search so that lawyers, research scholars, students and common masses can get the information expeditiously. It is accessible online. It has provision of citation search facility, filtering of retrieved records and online account o keep the selected record. It is also compliant with Web 2.0 tools and empowers users to contribute their own contents in the system.

Online Public Access Catalogue (OPAC)

1. "Online Public Access Catalogue (OPAC) is a computer based and supported library catalogue (bibliographic database) designed to be accessed via terminals so that the library users may directly and effectively search for and retrieve bibliographic records without the assistance human intermediary such as a specially trained member of the library staff" (ALA Glossary).

2. A public access online catalogue must, at minimums provide the bibliographic record content, retrieval functions and access points similar to, and understandable in terms of a card catalogue. Therefore the record content will include entry information, notes information and tracing information. The user must be able to locate, in the database, all works by an author, all editions or other versions of a work, all works on a given subject and a work or works with a specific title". (Kaske and Ferguson).

3. "A systematic record of holdings of collection, its purpose is to enable a user of the collection to find the physical location of information in the collection" (F. Kilgour).

Online Searching

It is the computer-assisted retrieval bibliographic citations. It means searching wherein the search is processed while the user is connected to the computer, thereby allowing the user to interact with the computer and adapt the search according to the computer's response. Since online is conducted as a two way conversation between the searcher and the system (Computer). The on line system is also called as interactive or conversational system (C.H. Penchell and T. H. Hogan).

Online Social Networking Tools (OSNT) – Benefits

The following are some of the important benefits of using SNT in delivery of library services. 1. *Providing reference assistance, library tours and promotes services,* 2. *Communicating and sending out information to the library users,* 3. *Help in teaching basic search tools,* 4. *Help in announcing programmes of the library and* 5. *Enable block posting of special selections to select library users.*

Ontology

1. A term used to denote the shared understanding of some domain of interest often conceived as a set of classes (concepts), relations, functions, axioms and instances. Ontologies are specifications of the conceptualization and the corresponding vocabulary used to describe a domain.
2. In Library and Information Science (LIS) context "it is the field of information management that basically defines a common vocabulary for users who need to share information in a domain" (V.A. Patkar).

Open Access (OA)

1. It means free and immediate availability on the public internet of those works which scholars give to the world without expectation of payment, permitting any user to

read, download, copy, , distribute, print, search or link to the full text of these articles, crawl them for any other lawful purpose.

2. OA is a worldwide movement where in full-text scholarly articles are completely free and un-restricted to all users to read, copy and download and distribute over the World Wide Web.

3. Literature; Its free availability on public internet, permitting any users to read, download, copy, distribute, print, search or link to the full texts of these articles crawl them for indexing, pass them as data to software or use them for any other lawful purpose, without financial, legal or technical barriers other than those inseparable from gaining access to the Internet itself" (Budapest Open Access Initiatives, 2001).

Features : 1. Open access literature in digital, 2. OA is compatible with copyright, Peer review, 3. OA campaign focuses on the literature that authors give to the world without expectation of payment, 4. OA literature is not free to publish or produce, 5. OA is compatible with peer review.

Types: 1. 'Green': the author can self-archive at the time of submission of the publication whether the publication is grey literature, a peer-reviewed journal publication, a peer-reviewed conference proceedings or monograph, 2. 'Gold': the author or author institution can pay a fee to the publisher at publication time, the publisher thereafter making the material available 'free' at the point of access.

Characteristics: 1. Cost of publication and distribution of articles is recovered from authors or institutions. 2. Access to publication in open access is more democratic, 3. The Author rather than the publisher own copyright in open access model, 4. Open access journals, like traditional journals, conduct peer review of submitted articles, and 5. Most of publishers of open access journals are non-profit, while a few are for profit. (e.g. Bio Med Central).

Resources : 1. Open Access Journals, 2. Open Access Books, 3. Open Access Courseware, 4. Open Access Institutional Repositories, 5. Open Access Electronic Theses and Dissertations, and 6. Open Access Databases.

Open Access Archives (OAA)

Open Access Archives or Repositories are digital collections of research articles that have been placed there by their authors. OA archives can be organized by discipline or institution. The primary goal of OA archiving is to maximize the accessibility of a research publications and their impact. OA archives can be limited e-prints or can include theses and dissertations, course material, institutional records or any other of digital file.

Open Access E-Book

An open access e-book book in electronic or digital form that is available on public internet free of charge, which can be read on a computer, laptop or e-book reader. Books are available in different web archives like digital depositories, databases and digital libraries, institutional repositories and offer creative possibilities for expanding access to information well as changing the learning behavior of user community.

Open Access Journals (OAJ)

These are scholarly journals that are available to the reader without financial or barrier other than access to internet itself. Some are subsidized and some require payment on behalf of the author. The subsidized ones are financed by an academic institution or government information centre.

Advantages : The content available to users everywhere regardless of affiliation with a subscribing library. This will benefit authors, academic readers, researchers, readers and general public and patients.

Objections : 1. Open access is unnecessary, 2. Open access is too impractical to implement.

Open Access Movement (OAM)

Started in the developing countries as a movement in recognition to the need that the output of public-funded research should be made available to the public at large without any barrier in relation to cost, access, etc., and dates back to 1991. The advent of Internet and its endless possibilities for information processing and distribution has been acting as a catalyst the growth of open access initiatives.

Open and Distance Learning (ODL)

It is a system wherein teachers and learners need not necessarily present either at the same place or same time and is flexible regarding modalities and timing of teaching and learning and also the admission criteria without compromising on necessary quality considerations. Recently it has become more useful for continuing education, skill development and quality education of relevance to learners located educationally disadvantageous locations.

Open Archival Information System (OAIS)

It is a reference model for achieving communities and most of the archiving projects are based on OAIS models. It specifies how digital assets should be preserve for users from the moment digital content is ingested into a digital storage area, through vigorous preservation, strategies to the creation of dissemination of packages for end users. The OAIS model was adopted as an ISO Standard CISO 14721 : 2003 OAIS.

Open Biblio

This is being developed by a small number of people and has been off and on again project. Development activity accelerated during 2006-2007 with the release of is 0.6.0 version. The latest version 0.7.1 has been released on March 18, 2012. This version has been recommended for new installations and updating older versions of open Biblio. The product includes cataloging, circulation and patron access catalog modules. The programming languages are PHP and LAMP and the operating system is Linux. UNIMARC is supported. There is an online demo and software can be downloaded.

Open Educational Resources (OER)

1. OER was defined as "the open provision of educational resources, enabled by information and communication technologies for consultation, use and adaptation by a community of users for non-commercial purposes" (UNESCO).
2. OECD defined OER as "digitized material offered freely and openly for educators, students and self-learners to use and reuse for teaching, learning and research".
3. OER are teaching, learning and research materials in any medium that reside in the public domain and have been released under an open license that permits access, use, repurposing, reuse and redistribution by others with no or limited restrictions.

This include: text-books, course material, modules, videos, tests, software and any other tools, materials or techniques used to support access to knowledge, audio-video lectures sound and music lesson plans, quizzes, syllabi, instructional modules, simulations, content, software tool, licenses and best practices (H. O. Chidinma).

Open Educational Resource (OER) Movement

It is the powerful idea that the world's knowledge is a public good. In addition there are many factors such as leveraging internet to freely share educational resources with the world, making education more affordable and accessible to students and revising content freely and legally to control courses and text-books in new and innovative ways that drive the academic community to participate in open education movement and to use OER in their courses.

Open J. Gate

It is an electronic gateway to global journal, literature in open access domain. Launched in 2006, Open J. Gate is the contribution of Informatics (India) Ltd., to promote OAI. Open J-Gate provides seamless access to millions of journal articles available online. Open J-Gate is also database of journal literature, indexed from 6082 open access journals, with links to full text at publisher sites.

Open Journal system (OJS)

It was developed in 2001 for managing and publishing scholarly journals online. OJS in an open source software for the management of peer reviewed academic journals released under GNU General Public License.

Features : 1. Installed locally and controlled locally, 2. Editors Configure requirements, sections and review process, 3. Online submission and management of all content, 4. Subscription module with delayed open access options, 5. Comprehensive indexing of the content, 6. Reading tools for content based on field and editor's choice, 7. Complete context sensitive online help and support.

Open Source Software (OSS)

This can be defined as computer software for which the human-readable source code is made available under a copyright license that meets the open source definition. This permits user to use, change and improve the software and to distribute it in modified or unmodified from.

Need : 1. Severe budget cuts, 2. Increased demand for services, 3. Lack of adequate staffing.

Characteristics : 1. Freely distributed, 2. Includes the source code, 3. Allows for derived works, 4. Maintain the integrity of the original source code, 5. No discrimination against persons or groups, 6. No discrimination against fields of endeavor, 7. Provides for distribution of the license, 8. Not

specific to a product, and 9. Not restricted to other softwares.
Advantages : 1. Software can be freely run for any purpose, 2. Software can be modified to the local needs, 3. Free to redistribute, 4. Modified versions can be freely circulated, 5. Source code can be freely distributed / circulated, 6. License will permit modifications and derived work of the software, 7. License will not restrict against any person or group, 8. License may not restrict about software usage, 9. License may be generic in nature, not specific to a particular product and 10. License must not contaminate other software by placing restrictions on it.

Disadvantages : 1. A library need to work more to adapt the software for the local needs, 2. Since open source soft-wares are developed on decentralized basis progress of problems can be confusing and there could be delays in addressing bugs, 3.Documenation tends to be limited and aimed at developers 4. It offers lesser level of customization when compared with proprietary software.

Operating System

An operating system is an organized collection of software that controls the overall operation of a computer. It enables the system's hardware to work with the user's application programmes. It allows users to load application program to primary storage section of a computer system. Operation system moves the data between primary and secondary storage units. It functions in many other ways unseen by the user.

Functions : 1. It makes a computer more convenient to use, 2. It allows the computer system resources to be used in an efficient manner. 3. It should be constructed in such a way as to permit the effective development, testing, and introduction of new system functions without at the same time interfering with service.

Optical Storage Devices

These are laser based mass storage devices that make possible faster access to information and saving of space. Of the various optical storage devices the following three devices find application in information storage and retrieval. 1. Compact Disc-Read-only memory (CD-ROM), 2. Write-once Optical Discs (WORM), 3. Erasable Optical Discs (EOD).

Organizational Security

An organizational security measure is done by calculating the sum value for the presence of procedures, controls, security policy, administrative tools and awareness creation.

Outsourcing

It is a tool to reduce costs and increase the quality of services. Many processes, functions and services in Libraries and Information Centres (LICs) are not done by the LICs staff members due to lack of staff and expertise in the specific processes or work. Further LICs want to concentrate on the core areas and thus not focus on multiple functions to simultaneously. It is seen as using expertise, skills, investment and infrastructure of third party sources to provide better services to the users at a low cost.

P

PANDORA

Means Preserving and Accessing Networked Documentary Resources of Australia and is an archive of copies of significant Australian online publications and websites issued on the internet. The National Library of Australia (NLA) and its partners are building the archive to assure long-term access to significant Australian documentary heritage that is published on line. PANDORA has been placed on the Memory of the World Australia Register in August 2004. The NLA selects e-journals from Australian Journal online database for preservation in PANDORA.

Pamphlet

It is an unbound booklet. It may consist of a single sheet of paper that is printed on both sides and folded in half, in thirds, or in fourths or it may consist of few pages that are folded in half and saddle stapled at the crease to make a simple book. According to UNESCO "a publication (other than periodical) to have at least 5 but not more than 48 pages exclusive of cover pages".

Patent

It is a time-limited, exclusive right granted for an invention. It is a temporary monopoly granted by the State to the owner of the invention. In return for the disclosure of the details of the invention, the owner is given the sole right to its exploitation. The invention may be a new product, or a process and the patent protects the owner / inventor from others who may attempt to make, use, distribute or sell the invention without the parent owner's consent.

Patent documents

These represent the most promising data in terms of being most structured, systematic and updated. These shall have abundant information about developed technology which includes title, abstract, claims, inventors and drawings, date of publication and date of grant.

Pay-Per-View Model

This model is equivalent to paid document delivery service. Publishers never offered this model in the print world. Digital content has made this model a new though very limited revenue opportunity for the publishers and a strategy to protect the stable revenue from subscription model. This model has all the potential to bloom as a cost affordable option to both libraries and end-users.

Performance Appraisal (PA)

1. This process of evaluation or assessment of performance of an individual or of an institution, keeping in view the objectives of the parent organization and the consequent application is known as performance appraisal.
2. "Any procedure which helps he collecting, checking, sharing, giving and using of information collected from and about people at work for the purpose of adding to their performance of work" (Randol et.al)

Techniques of Performance Appraisal : 1. Annual Confidential Report, 2. Self-Assessment, 3. Interview Schedule, 4. Appraisal by Clientele, 5. Management by Objectives (MBO).

Merits : 1. It opens up another channel of communication between the employees, 2. It provides an opportunity to review the content of job within an organization and to assess their relevance, 3. It provides a method of detecting the need for and of managing change, 4. The performance appraisal schemes concentrate on the person in a particular job, 5. An organization has a record of all staffs' achievements constantly available for planning, promotion and writing references.

Demerits : 1. Many managers are not capable of apprising their staff, 2. Many staff members may feel aggrieved at their staff appraisal interviews, 3. Appraisal is always to subjective opinion, 4. Staff appraisals sometimes become sterile.

Objectives : 1. Monitor efforts of an individual, 2. Integrate and coordinate an individual's efforts into a cooperative endeavor, 3. Provide protection and feedback to an individual, 4. Provides means of correcting or commending the efforts of an individual and 5. Provides an equitable consistent basis of distributing rewards and penalties (M. L. Monga).

Purpose : 1. Administrative decisions i.e. promotion, transfers and allocation financial rewards, 2. Employee development i.e. identification of training needs, performance feedback, 3. Personnel research i.e. generation of manpower information for salary and wage determination, career planning, man-job matching, promotion, etc.

Performance Appraisal Evaluation

It is an ongoing process which includes a clear definition of employees' duties and responsibilities, the establishment of performance standards and a reasonable understanding of expectations and goal. It is a formal procedure by which the librarian and supervisor improve communication, promote team effort in the unit, foster professional development of the library staff and determine performance level.

Performance Assessment (PA)

It is a systematic and objective internal and or external evaluation of library design, implementation and results of ongoing or completed activities, project, program or policy with the aim of determining the efficiency, effectiveness, impact and sustainability of the library's programmes. In essence performance assessment focuses on critical resources, expertise, equipment and supplies needed to implement the planned activities of a library. (A. M. Tammaro)

Performance Evaluation (PE)

It is a formal procedure by which the librarian and supervisor improve communication, promote team effort in the unit / department, foster professional development of the library staff and determine performance / merit level. The most important considerations of performance evaluation are the level of performance based on job description and the achievement of annual goals of the library / information centre.

Objectives : 1. To work towards achievement of the mission goals and objectives of the library / information centre, 2. To inform the staff of their strengths, weaknesses and progress, 3. To improve individual and team performance and productivity, 4. To strengthen work relationships and improve communication, 5. To develop employees skills, 6. To recognize accomplishments and good work of employees, 7. To recommend deserved employee/s for merit promotion and 8. To find out training needs of employee/s.

Performance Indicators (PIs)

According to Christine Abbot "PI is a quantitative expression of the use or value of an aspect of library service". The terms Performance measurement, Performance analysis and Performance Indicators are used interchangeably in relation to aims and objectives.

Performance Standards

"A means of measuring the quantity of work produced by a person working at a normal pace under normal condition" (Dougherty and Heinritz)

Usefulness : 1. Provide an objective basis for decisions, 2. Offer a factual basis upon which to balance workload and personnel, 3. Aid in selecting from among two or more means, 4. Providde an objective test for the relative effectiveness of new methods, 5. Strengthen the personnel programe, 6. Form the basis for balancing work related functions, 7. Aid in predicting future budget needs and 8. Offer the basis for determining the cost of a proposed project (Tuttle).

Perpetual Access Rights

This model is similar to libraries buying books and journals in the print model. The library can license the content that grants access rights by its user community for unlimited period. Technically this means that the library has the access rights for its organizational life.

Personal Archive

It is to deposit a digital document in a publicly accessible website preferably an DAI compliant that involves a simple web interface where the depositor prepare the metadata and then attaches the full text document.

Personal Blog

It is an online diary or journal such as blogger or live journal. It is a space for users to write their day-to-day experiences, complaints, thoughts and many more. The weblog formats usually user-friendly and all own inexperienced bloggers to create, format and post entries easily.

Personal Competencies

These include a set of skills, attitudes and values that enable library and information professionals to work efficiently, be good communicators, focus on continuing learning throughout their career, demonstrate the value added nature of their contributions and strive for survival in the competitive environment.

Personal Computers

Personal Computer(s) is a general purpose micro computer system that executes program instructions to perform a wide variety of tasks. These come in many shapes and sizes. Some are note book size or smaller and weigh less than four pounds. Other briefcase size portables weigh a little more. These are designed to be used by one person at a time and that is, they are single user oriented.

Personality [P]

The fundamental category 'Personality' [P] is the most

crucial, important and essential category among the five fundamental categories (FFC). Ranganathan has not attempted to define the fundamental category personality. He felt 'Personality' to represent the focal point of description or key object or objects of study or description of a work. E.g. Public Library. In the main class (MC) Library Science Public Library is personality.

Personal Library

It is a library under the care of private ownership, as compared to that of a public institution, and it is usually established only for the use of a small number of people, or even a single person. It is owned and maintained by individuals for their exclusive use. "Personal library is a considerable collection of books kept for use and not as merchandise, as a private library" or "a building or apartment appropriated for holding such a collection of books" (Webster's Dictionary).

Photo blog

It is photo sharing sites such as Buzznet and Flickr. They integrated the typical photo gallery service with photo sharing, blogging and syndication to create a new kind of social networking.

Photocopier

A Photo Copier is a machine that makes paper copies of documents and other visual image quickly and cheaply. Most current photocopiers use a technology called xerography, a dry process using heat. Photocopying is widely use in libraries.

Physical library

The term emphasizes the values of libraries as physical spaces where users gather to use and borrow library materials in different media to acquire information and at that time they often seek assistance of a helpful librarian. , Conventional circulation system is an example.

Physical Security

It indicates that unauthorized access to into library building, leading, theft or vandalism threats in a particular library or information centre. This includes physical security features, user identification and authentication entrance and exits, window security, door protection security, etc.

Plagiarism

1. It means lifting of research papers, reports, etc. directly from the Internet and submitting them without acknowledging the sources. Mostly academics face this problem frequently. Many research publications and even Ph.D. theses are just copied or lifted and submitted to learned periodicals like *Nature, Science, ACM Communication* as well as whistle blowers like Society for Scientific Values (India).

2. According to Fishman "Plagiarism occurs when someone: *1. Uses words, ideas, or work products, 2. Attributable to another identifiable person or source, 3. Without attributing the work to the source from which was obtained, 4. In a situation in which there is a legitimate expectation of original authorship and 5. To obtain some benefit, credit or gain which need to be monetary.*

   Seven deadly sins of Plagiarism: 1. Failure to provide credit, 2. Copying material from Internet without citing it, 3. Failure to cite even a few words of borrowed language, 4. Failure to cite an exact quote, 5. Failure to cite paraphrased ideas, 6. Failure to provide an accurate citation and 7. Thinking one can get away with plagiarism (Kaust Library, Saudi Arabia).

Planning (in relation to Information system or Centre)

It is the dynamic process of committing resources systematically and with the best possible knowledge of the future; of organizing systematically the effort needed to utilize these resources, and of measuring results of planning decisions against expectations through systematic feedback.

Advantages: 1. Helps systematically move towards the achievement of goals, 2. Helps to identify and differentiating the essential priority actions and not so essential actions, 3. Helps bring about concerted and cohesive action by a group of people, 4. Helps re-checking, error-identifying and re-modifying due to unforeseen circumstances, 5. Helps in clear demarcation and allocation of activities among a group of people, 6. Helps to draft a financially elastic budget and 7. Provides an integrated and yet analytical projection of a future course of action of a centre. (P. Atherton).

Platform as a Service(PaaS)

Cloud computing has evolved to include platforms for building and running custom applications, a concept known as 'platform as service' (or Paas). PaaS applications are also referred to as on-demand, web based or software as a service (or SaaS) solution. In this a computing platform supplies tools and a development environment to help organizations to build, test and deploy web-based applications.

Plone

It is a free and open source content management system built on top of the Zope application server. Plone is released under the GNU General Public License (GPL) and is designed to be extensible Additional functionality is added to Plone with products which may be distributed through Plone Website or otherwise. Some important features: *Collaboration and sharing, Workflow capabilities, Presentation mode for content, Wiki support, Time based publishing, Human readable URLS, Powerful graphical page editor, Navigation and updated site maps, Accessibility complaint, Free add-on products, Cross-platforms, and Backup support.*

Political blog or Watch blog

It is usually the comments posted by an individual that link articles from new websites. It usually sets out to criticize what the author considers systematic errors or bias in an online newspaper or news site. These days politicians also use blog to run their campaign e.g. presidential campaign of Barack Obama of America during 2008.

Portal

1. "A website that aims to be an entry point to the World Wide Web, typically offering search engine and / or links to useful pages and possibly news or other services. These services are usually provided for free in the hope that their users will make the site their default home page or a last visit it often" (The Internet Dictionary).
2. "A network service that brings together content from diverse distributed resources using technologies such as cross searching, harvesting and altering, and collects this into an amalgamated form for presentation via a web browser to the user" (The Joint Information System Committee).

Core functions: 1. Browsable (by subject) and searchable database of available resources, 2. Cross-searching of multiple resources, 3. Use of open URL to carry the use through form hits in bibliographic database to ways to access the appropriate copy of the full text or document delivery options.

Portico

It is a digital preservation service provided by IHAKA, a not-for-profit organization with a mission to help the academic community to use digital technologies to preserve the scholarly record and to advance research and teaching in sustainable ways. Portico was started in 2002 to create a sustainable digital archive. It has collaborated with 151 publishers and 741 libraries to archive 13,690 and 129,890 e-journals and e-books.

Power Point Presentation

A power point presentation is a collection of slides, handouts, speaker's notes, outline all in one file. Slides are the individual pages of presentation. Handouts consist of smaller printed versions of slides either 2, 3 or 6 per page. The speaker's notes will contain a small image of the slide on each notes page, along with brief notes on the notes pages. The Microsoft Power Point is one of the most popular presentation graphics software that comes with Microsoft office. The PowerPoint can be used for producing professional looking presentat with features like text handing, outlining drawing, graphing, clip art, etc.

Precision and Recall

Precision is the number of documents that are relevant to a query while Recall is the number of truly relevant documents that are effectively retrieved. Precision is a measure of soundness of the IR System while Recall provides a measure of completeness of the system (S. Kohli and A. Gupta)

Predatory Journal(s)

These journals earn their revenue through huge article processing charges from authors. They invite papers with assurance such as "quick reviewing process" and "fast publication". Another fact is the non-transparent "peer review" / no review process in predatory journals that allow papers to accepted without any change. This is a big challenge for developing country like India, as many low quality papers are getting published.

Preservation

The term "Preservation" includes all actions that can be taken with the aim of ensuring the current and long-term survival and accessibility of the physical form, information content and relevant metadata of archival records, including actions taken to influence records creators prior to acquisition or selection" (National Archives of Australia).

Primary Documents

Documents as they are produced by the author, that is, the original carrier of information.

Print-on-Demand (PoD)

It is a new method of printing books which allows books to be printed one a time or on demand. This method helps free publishers from the process of doing a traditional print runoff thousands of books at a time. The technology involves complex laser printing systems and electronically formatted text, which the printers can read. Many publishers including Web upstarts, are hopping this method will allow them to more effectively print smaller number of books and still make a profit.

Project Gutenberg

It is the first largest single collection of free e-books. Michael Hart the brain behind this project which was started in 1971 feels that anything that can be entered into a computer can be reproduced indefinitely. The project currently offers free download of 38,000 e-books in the public domain all digitized by volunteers. In the years to come, it aims to make available 10 million books in 100 languages. It hosts a lot of books on Indian history, philosophy, literature, flora and fauna of India.

Promotion of Library Automation and Networking in North Eastern Region(PLANER)

It is a special initiative taken up by Information and Library Network (INFLIBNET) Centre to bring awareness among library professionals in the field of information technology and its application to library services. INFLIBNET has so far successfully organized seven such PLANNERS indifferent parts of North East in collaboration with the Universities located in region on rotation basis in each State.

Public Information Kiosks

It is an action research project of National Institute of Rural Development and Panchayat Raj (NIRD), Hyderabad, which works as an information cum communication centre.

Objectives : 1. Awareness building about rural development programs, 2. Database development on the resources of the local area, 3. Information and Communication services, and 4. Empowering citizens with information.

Programs: 1. Clean and Green program, 2. Development of Women and Children in Rural Areas, 3. Employment Assurance Scheme and 4. Janmabhoomi.

Public Kiosks

These are known as 'tele-centres' 'Internet Cafes' or 'Multipurpose community information and communication centres'. These can be owned privately or publicly like in schools, libraries or NGO offices, etc. These are very effective in countries like India where computer density as well as information literacy is very low.

Public Library

"It is a public library which being the local gateway to knowledge, provides basic condition for lifelong learning, independent decision making and cultural development of the individual and social groups; a living force for education, culture and information, an essential agent for fostering of peace and spiritual welfare through the minds of men and women;the local center of information, making all kinds of knowledge information readily and freely available to its users; accessible for all, regardless of age, race, sex, religion, nationality, language or social status, and lastly, the libraries which have collections and services, all types of appropriate media and modern technologies as well as traditional materials with high quality and have relevance to local needs and conditions. Material must reflect current trends and the evolution of society as well as memory of human endeavor and imagination". (UNESCO Public Library Manifesto).

Basic Objectives : 1. To serve as an instrument of education for the development of self in particular and the society in general, irrespective of the level of education and to act as a bridge between the person and the knowledge recorded in documents, 2. To provide up-to-date and correct information on topical issues, 3. To act as cultural centres, encouraging public participation, taste for library and cultural actives and promotion of fine arts, 4. To enable the public to use their leisure time constructively and to provide wholesome recreative reading material.

Public Relations

"It is the deliberate, planned and sustained effort to establish and maintain mutual understanding between an organization and its public". (British Institute of Public Relations).

Kinds : 1. Institutional Relation; 2. Press Relations; 3. Service Relations; 4. User Relations; 5. Media Relations; 6. Customer Relations; and 7. Clientele Relations.

Publish or Perish (PoP)

This was created by Anne-WilHarzingto assist faculty looking for more diverse bibliometrics. It is a free and downloadable program that harvests data from Google Scholar based on author names. Users can manually remove records to refine the data, just similar to what is now offered by Google Scholar Citations.

Pub Med Central

It is a free archive of biomedical and life sciences journal literature at the US National Institutes of Health's National Library of Medicine (NIH / NLM). In keeping with NML's legislative mandate to collect and preserve the biomedical literature, the PMC serves as a digital counterpart of NML's extensive print journal collection. It was launched in February 2000 and is managed by NML's National Centre for Biotechnology information (NCBI). As an archive PMC is designed to provide permanent access to all of its content, even as technology evolves and current digital literature formats potentially become obsolete. It provides access to more than 250 journals from 50+ publishers. It regains all perpetual rights to archive all submitted materials and aims at maintaining the long-term integrity and accuracy of the contents.

Q

Quality of Work Life (QWL)

Walton defined QWL "as a process by which an organization responds to employees needs for developing mechanism to allow them to share fully in making decisions that design their lives at work".

Quality Management (QM)

"Managing the entire organization, so that it exceeds in all dimensions of products and services which are important to the customers. Excellence in a QM Organization is defined by customer requirements and needs". (Rowley).

It is concerned with integration of all efforts in the organization towards quality and customer case. Benefits of quality management in libraries: 1. *Incremental changes leading to continuous improvement,* 2. *Motivates library managers to develop leadership skills to achieve good results,* 3. *Enhances staff participation in decision making,* 4. *Increases the abilities and skills of Library Staff,* 5. *Provides a method of improving services to users,* and 6. *The time utilized to provide information services to user community decreases while the efficiency increases.*

Quality Management System (QMS)

As per ISO 9001 QMS guides library administrators to coordinate and allocate resources as well as provide support for technical services and clients' services to satisfy customer's needs and helps in evaluating service performance at a regular interval and continually improve the quality of library services.

Quick Response (QR) Code

It is two dimensional barcodes. It was first designed in Japan for automobile industry. Now the QR code is very common in mobile phone web industry. The website's address is easily transformed in to QR code by various software. These QR codes are quickly read by mobile phone devices. The QR codes are very helpful rather than typing web addresses on small phone devices. These are more useful than barcode because they can store much more data.

R

RFID (Radio Frequency Identification)

It is a wireless data collection technology that uses electronics for storing data. Like barcodes, they are used to identify items. --Unlike barcodes which must be brought close to the scanner for reading, RFID tags are read when they are within the proximity of a transmitted radio signal.

Dictionary of Library and Information Science defines RFID as "the use of microchips to tag library materials and library card, enabling patrons to checkout item by walking through a self-service station equipped with an antenna that emits low frequency radio waves".

Application in Libraries : 1. Annual stock taking, 2. Rapid checking that books are shelved in the correct area, 3.

Searching for specific items using a scanner, 4. Self-check-out items, 5. Security and 6. Library membership cards.

Components of an RFID System 1. RFID tags that are electronically programmed with unique information, 2. Readers or sensors to query the tags, 3. Antenna and 4. Server on which the software that interfaces with the integrated library software is loaded.

RFID Systems

RFID (Radio Frequency Identification) Security systems are commonly used in the present library environment. These RFID based security systems are designed to improve the library operations efficiently. These systems will detect the unauthorized check-out of reading material when the users did not present them for borrowing to the circulation desk. The EM(Electro Magnetic) Tags which are activated to the RFID systems are required to insert in the books and other reading materials.

Advantages : 1. Reduction in the amount of time required to perform circulation operations, 2. Simplified user self-charging and discharging, 3. Highly reliable, 4. High speed inventorying, 5. Automatic materials handling and 6. Long-tag-life.

Rackspace Cloud

It is a cloud computing platform that offers three types of services for organizations and businesses viz: Cloud servers, cloud files and cloud balances. Cloud services are available to organizations in different sizes and are measured by the amount of physical memory reserved for an instance and range from 256 MB upto 30 GB on operating system of their choice to run various web services.

Readability

"The quality of or capacity for, being read with pleasure or interest, considered as measured by certain assessable factor, as case of comprehension, alternativeness and style"

(The Oxford English Dictionary, 2nd Edn.).

Readability Issues : "1. Legibility of print of books / documents, 2. Alternative formats, 33. Illustrations and color, 4. Motivation on reader's factors, 5. Comprehension, 6. Conceptual difficulties, 7. Vocabulary, 8. Syntactic Structures, 9. Organization of the narration or discourse, 10, Style of Writing, and 11. Reading Speed". (L. S. Ramaiah).

Reading

It is a multidimensional cognitive process of decrypting symbols to build and develop meaning from the recommended text and the context. There are no concrete rules for reading, rather reading permits readers to produce or reproduce their own ideas introspectively. It is a way of semantic acquirement, communication, distribution of information and thoughts.

Objectives : 1. To satisfy one curiosity, 2. To broader perspective of knowledge / information, 3. To up-to-date knowledge in respect of current development, 4. To get acquainted with the heritage of one's own country, 5. To develop critical outlook, thinking and to possess mature judgment, and 6. To attain spiritual solace.

Real-time search

1. It means "looking through material that literally is published in real-time. In other words, material where there is practically no delay between composition and publishing". (Danny Sullivaan).
2. "Finding the right answer to your question based on what is available right now, about the subject you care about right now. Real time search is finding the Right Answer, Right now" (Kimbal Musk).

Reasons of Marketing

The major reasons of adopting marketing strategies for

library services are: 1. Attracting funding agencies, 2. Showcase the potential of libraries and attract users, 3. Image enhancement, 4. Relevancy in the digital age and 5. Recognition of Library and Library profession in society (Okon and Umoh).

Records and Archives Management Programme (RAMP)

The Division of the General Information Programme (PGI) of UNESCO launched this programme with the following objectives: 1. Promote formulation of information policies and plans (national, regional and international), 2. Promote and disseminate methods, norms and standards for information handling, 3. Contribute to the development of information infrastructure, 4. Contribute to the development of specialized information systems and 5. Promote the training and education of specialists in and users of information.

Referral Centre

The indication of sources (persons, institutions, publications, etc.) from which scientific information may be obtained on a given subject.

Functions : 1. To collect, on a worldwide basis, information about data and information resources within the subject or mission, 2. To prepare a comprehensive inventory of the kinds of data / information / services available from these services, 3. To guide users for the appropriate sources of the required data or information.

Reference Service

1. According to Dr. S. R. Ranganathan Reference Service is "Personal service to each reader in helping him to find the documents answering his interest at the moment pin pointedly, exhaustively and expeditiously".
2. ALA Glossary of Library Terms defines Reference Service as "that phase of library work which is directly concerned with assistance to readers in securing

information and in using resources of the library in study and research.

Need for reference service: 1. Users' day to day information needs and demand for intensive search service, 2. Complexities in the growth and explosion of knowledge and growth of libraries, 3. Modern tools and techniques and methods employed by various types of libraries, 4. Volume, variety and complexity of documents and 5. Impact of Information and communication technologies.

Regional Bibliographical Control(RBC)

It means systematic record of all published materials such as books, periodicals and other reading materials including non-book materials published in the languages and emanating from the region of the country. For example in the context of India it is the five Southern States of India viz: *Telangana, Andhra Pradesh, Tamil Nadu, Karnataka and Kerala.*

Relationship Marketing (RM)

It is the approach to build relationships with users. R.M. cultivates the relationship among users and staff. It help in retaining the existing users and enhances loyalty among staff. R.M. uses ICT to contact and communicate more easily with library users and potential users in the society.

Repository

1. It refers to a location for storage, often for safety or preservation. It supports mechanisms to import, export, identify, store, preserve and retrieve digital assets.
2. It is a collection of resources that can be accessed to retrieve information. Repositories often consist of several databases tied together by a common search engine.

Types: 1. Digital, Institutional, and 3. Open Access.

Benefits : 1. Attracting new staff and students to institutions, 2. Increased transparency and quality of learning materials, 3. Sharing expertise within institutions, 4. Supports storage, management, preservation and retrieval content, 5. Facilitates availability of resources to accredited bodies, 6. Repository content is readily searchable both locally and globally, 7. Repositories also store grey literature which is not necessarily published, 8. Repositories could provide cost savings in the long run, 9. Offers greater flexibility over websites with better security and preservation of various kinds of digital material.

Reprint

It is that position of a publication, journal, conference proceedings of seminars which is distributed by author on private basis, consists of the full-fledge document right from the title to reference, such reprints are generally supplied in multiple copies by the publishers to the authors.

Advantages : 1. Quack access, 2. Time saving, 3. Feedback, 4. Network, 5. Cited ness, 6. Personal library and 7. Economical.

Reprography

1. The term reprography was coined in the 1960s which has generally been referred to document reproduction techniques. It is a process of obtaining a copy of a required document. It can be Xerography, scanning, digital printing and photography. Among all, the reprography is the most popular technique used in our society for document reproduction.
2. "The Branch of technology concerned with the copying and reproduction of documentary and graphic material" (OED).
3. "The technology of producing and reproducing two dimensional visual communication media in business

and administrative operation" (Institute of Administrative Management).

4. "The field which deals with techniques and problems of document production in a variety of forms e.g. duplication, photo-copying and micro-copying" (UNISIST Working Document).

Research

"Studious enquiry or examination; specifically and usually, critical and exhaustive investigation having for its aim the discovery of new facts and their correct interpretation, the revision of accepted conclusions, theories or laws, in the light of newly discovered facts or the practical applications of such new or revised conclusions, etc.". (Webster's New International Dictionary).

Objectives : 1. To find new generalization with new data, 2. To know old conclusions with new data, 3. To attempt to reach more conclusions from the same set of data, 4. To put forward an entirely original idea or theory or to discover an unexplored horizon of knowledge, 5. To find out or resolve contradictions existing in the area of study, and 6. To continuously develop a discipline or field of study with the use of scientific and rational methods.

Research Data

It is the data which is generated when a researcher undertakes or executes any research activity or project. Research data is generated across all fields of study i.e., Sciences, Social Sciences and Humanities, etc. The data may be textual, quantitative, qualitative, images, recordings, numerical compositions, verbal communication, experimental readings simulations and codes.

Research Gate

It is an academic social network site designed primarily for scholars to create their own profiles upload their scholarly work and communicating among peers.

Resource Description and Access (RDC)

RDC was built on the foundations established by the Anglo-American Cataloguing Rules (AACR) and provides a comprehensive set of guidelines and instructions on resource description and access covering all types of content and media.

Resource Sharing

"Resource sharing in its most positive aspects entails reciprocity implying partnership in which each member has something useful to contribute to others and which each is willing and contribute to others and which each is willing and able to make available when needed" (Allen Kent).

Important areas of resource sharing : 1. Resource sharing in acquisition, 2. Centralized cataloguing, 3. National Union Catalogue, 4. Computerized network for resource sharing and 5. Preservation of library materials.

Resource sharing via network implies automation, data communication and effective cooperation. Sharing of resources is an important factor in automation and networking which have come into being.

Need : 1. Increasing cost of documents, 2. Explosion of knowledge and growth in document production, 3. Shrinking library budget, 4. To reduce operational cost of libraries, 5. Advent of technological solutions, 6. Meeting user satisfaction and 7. To optimise utilization of existing document resources.

Responsible Research and Innovation (RRI)

It is a "transparent interactive processes by which societal actors and innovations become mutually responsive to each other with a view on the (ethical) acceptability, sustainability and social desirability of the innovation process and its marketable products (in order to allow a proper embedding of scientific and technological advances in society)". (R. Von Schomberg).

Retail Informatics

It is a technique, approach and procedure as well as domain for management and manipulation of information and content of business community including retailer, wholesaler, agencies, third parties general shop, common user and customer and so on. It is actually integrating Information Science and retail management. It is mainly dedicated to computer tools and technologies which is needed to store and process data.

Retrospective Conversion (RECON)

It is the process of converting manual bibliographic records to machine-readable files suitable for use with a computer based library system. Such a conversion activity needs n appropriate standard to convert a record along in the proper relationship to the entire automation project. Technological advances have facilitated fast access to information at various levels. Standardized records reduce the chances of error and increase the capabilities of remote access, searching and retrieval through network configuration.

Advantages : 1. The need for labour-intensive physical cataloguing is a limited, 2. Standardised records reduce the chance of errors or inconsistencies, 3. Easy to locate current and accurate information, 4. Increase remote access capabilities.

Retrospective Conversion of Library Catalogue

It means the conversion of library existing bibliographic records from manual to machine-readable format according to specified policies and standards.

Review Literature

It involves locating, reading and evaluating reports of research as well as reports of casual observation and opinion that are related to individual planned research projects (Borg and Gall).

Right to Information

It means an individual's rights to know about the governmental activities, the proposals, projects, the way they are going to be implemented, the funds that are being raised, the way they are being spent, the purpose and objectives of legislation, the way they are interpreted, opportunities made available to the public for their economic growth of development.

The Right to Information Act, 2005 explains the meaning and scope of the phrase at Sec.2 (F) as follows:

"Right o information means the right to information accessible under this Act which is held by or under the control of any public authority to:

(i) Inspection of work, documents or records;
(ii) Taking notes, extracts or Certified copies of documents or records;
(iii) Taking certified copies of materials;
(iv) Obtaining information in the form of diskettes, floppies, tapes, videocassettes or in any other electronic mode or through printouts where such information is stored on a computer or in any other device".

The Right to Information Act ((2005)

The Parliament of India has passed the Right to Information (RTI) Act in May 2005. This Act, which received Presidential assent in June 2005, came into force from 13th October, 2005. The passing of this Act is truly a landmark occasion. For the first time, after independence, the citizens of India have a real opportunity to exercise this very important right. Under the provision of the Act, any citizen (including citizens within J & K) may request information from 'Public authority' (a body of Government or instrumentality of State) which is required to reply expeditiously or within thirty days.

Right to Libraries

American Library Association (ALA) issued a declaration in 2013 for the Right to Libraries which serves as a strong public statement about the value of libraries for individuals, communities and their nation (ALA, 2013). In the document it has been stated that "....libraries are essential to a democratic society. Every day in countless communities across our nation and the world millions of children, students and adults use libraries to learn, grow and achieve their dreams. In addition, to a vast array of books, computers and other resources, library users benefit from the expert teaching and guidance of librarians and library staff to help their minds and open new worlds". The declaration further advocates for the value of libraries as:

1. Libraries empower the individual; 2. Libraries support literary and life-long learning; 3. Libraries strengthen families, 4. Libraries are the greatest equalizer, 5. Libraries build communities, 6. Libraries protect our right to know, 7. Libraries strengthen our nation, 8. Libraries advance research and scholarship, 9. Libraries helps to better understand each other, 10. Libraries preserve our Nation's cultural heritage.

Risk Management

It is the process of measuring or assessing risk and then developing strategies to manage the risk. It is based on assessment; every risk management includes a number of tasks viz. *1. Identification of concerns, 2. Identification of risks, 3. Evaluation of the risks as to likelihood and consequences, 4. Assessment of options for accommodating the risks, 5. Prioritization of risk management efforts and 6. Development of risk management plans.*

Rural Community Resource Centres

According to Shirley Giggey " ....Is a place where means of a community can – find information about subjects of interest to them, — take part in learning activities, discuss and share knowledge, information and concerns with extension and other community workers, planners and administrators, find materials to help them retain their literacy and numeracy skills, meet to organize and work together on common community projects, use equipment to produce their own information materials – enjoy cultural and leisure activities".

S

SCOPUS

It is one of the most popular citation indexes among the academic, research and the scientific community across the world. The database has more than 22000 journals indexed with it. The SCOPUS database titles include book series, conference proceedings and journal titles.

SLIM21

It is designed and developed by Algorithms Consultants (P) Ltd. The Acronym for SLIM is System for Library Information Management. The first version of SLIM software was launched in the year 1988. Since then, it has been continuously improved by incorporating feedback from clients and adapting to the latest technical innovations. SLIM21 is an ISO 9000 compliant. 2008 Certified Company. SLIM21 has various modules for capturing information on books, e-books, films, sound recordings, drawing, clippings, articles, reports, pamphlets, serial publications, etc., These modules cover the complete functionality required for automating libraries such as cataloguing, acquisition, serial control, circulation, etc.

SOUL (Software for University Libraries)

The Integrated Library Management Software, SOUL has been designed and developed by INFLIBNET for library automation. This is user friendly software which operates on windows and works under client server architecture. The first version as released under CALIBER 2000. The latest version of the software i.e. SOUL 2.00 was released in 2009. The database for new version of SOUL is designed under the latest version of MS-SQL and My-SQL. Various international standards of networking, bibliographic and circulation protocols are being followed by the SOUL Software.

SOUL 2.0

Software for University Libraries (SOUL) is state-of-the-art integrated management software designed and developed by the INFLIBNET Centre based on requirements of college and University libraries. The latest version of the software is SOUL 2.0 was released in January 2009.

STRIDE (Scheme for Trans disciplinary Research for India's Developing Economy)

The UGC has announced the new scheme called STRIDE in order to promote trans disciplinary research in the Country. The Scheme was launched on July 1, 2019.

Main objectives : To identify young talent, strengthen research, culture, build capacity, promote innovation and support inter-disciplinary research for India's developing economy and national development.

SUPLIS (Supreme Court Library Information System)

Computerisation process in the Supreme Court started in 1992. Supreme Court Judges' Library has introduced new technology in phased manner with three distinct projects under its planned programme viz: *1. Case Indexing, 2. Current Contents (Academic articles) and 3. Legislation.* The Judges' Library identified the database of about 25,000 decided cases from 1950 onwards and approximately 1500 cases reportable / non-reportable annually. Library database SUPLIS was programmed on the Hardware XENIX 486. SUPLIS was retrieval mechanism developed on the SUPLIS was retrieval mechanism developed on the basis information seeking needs of users. This system has been created on the basis of queries and requisition received from the courts, court officials, different departments of the court and Hon'ble judges.

SUSHI (Standardized Usage Statistics Harvesting Initiative)

The National Information Standards Organization (NISO) has come up with standardized usage Statistics Harvesting Initiative (SUSHI) Protocol, which defines an automated request and response model for harvesting of electronic resource usage data utilizing a web services framework. The SUSHI standard is built on SOAP (Simple Object Access Protocol) which takes the users details as SOAP request and gives the usage report in XML format as a response.

SWAYAM

Government of India launched an indigenous programme named Study Webs of Active Learning for Young Aspirant Minds with an objective to serve, to serve a huge domain of learners as well as the demands of a knowledge economy and society.

Sanjay

It is a library automation software package which has been designed and developed by DESIDOC, Delhi with the support of NISSAT by augmenting CDS / ISIS (Ver. 2.3) to cater to the need of library management. Special features are: *1. User-friendly for library housekeeping operations, 2. Has a set of 70 Pascal programmes and 25 special menus, 3. Faster response time, 4. Effective interlinking of database and 5. Modified CDS / ISIS augmented to cover several additional applications. The package was marketed by NISSAT New Delhi at a nominal price.*

Scholarly Communication

It is often used interchangeably with the term scholarly publishing. It is the process of academics, scholars and researchers sharing and publishing their research findings so that they are available to the wider academic community and beyond. It includes both the dissemination and access to scholarship and research in a variety of formats and states of completion, such as published books or journal articles, research results and data sets and drafts of papers (Wikipedia).

Forms: Kling and Callahan have identified the following forms of scholarly communication.

1. Social and socio-technical research literature like e-journals, research monographs, specialized research conference.
2. Technological research literature which includes analytical examination of technological standards and design strategies.
3. Practioner literature where primary audience includes publishers, librarians, academic administrators and faculty who may publish in e-media, organize electronic collections, evaluate such electronic publications, and
4. Scholarly electronic forms.

Scholarly Content

It implies formally published scholarly literature, in particular journal articles and conference proceedings, editorial documents and doctoral dissertations, the contents of institutional repositories. It may also include pre-prints and other works in progress, peer reviewed articles monographs, conference papers, electronic theses and dissertations, and grey literature.

Science Citation Index (SCI)

In 1955 Eugene Garfield, the father of citation Indexing, revolutionised the concept scientific research with his concept of citation Indexing and searching. In 1961 *Science Citation Index* (SCI) was published including 562 journals and 2 million citations. Over the year SCI transformed from print form to online with the Dialog in the 1970's, CD-ROM in 1980's and finally a web interface in 1997. In due course the content was enhanced and *Social Sciences Citation Index* was released in 1973 covering journals from 1956, the *Arts & Humanities Citation Index* was released in 1978 covering journals from 1975 and *Century of Science* in 2004 covering Science Journals back to 1900.

Scientific Method

"A collective term denoting the various processes by the aid of which the sciences are built-up" (Encyclopaedia Britannica). In a wider sense any method of investigation by which scientific o other impartial and systematic knowledge is acquired is called scientific method. It involves the following methods. *1. Identification of a problem, 2. Formation of a hypothesis, 3. Collection of all possible data and verification of hypothesis, and 4. Generalization.*

Scientific Publication

Any kind of written material carrying scientific and technological information either as print or electronic resources. The major forms of these publications include research reports, books, conference proceedings, patents, primary and secondary journals. Less important are research notes and letters, etc. Among these varied forms, online journals and C-Databases are the most frequently used sources of data.

Scientometrics

1. "It is a science of the application of mathematical and statistical methods which are often developed to measure and evaluate the scientific publications". It is utilised to identify the pattern of publication,

authorship, productive author, author affiliation, year wise growth, citations and behaviour of a subject over a period of time and thereby offering insight into the dynamics of the area under study which in turn help to formulate a science policy. (S. Ashwathy and A. GopiKuttan).

2. It is a discipline which analyses scientific publications and citations appended to the paper to gain an understanding of the structure of science, growth of Science at global level, performance of country in a particular domain, performance of institutions, departments / divisions and scientific eminence of an individual scientist. It also helps in knowing the information seeking behaviour of scientists and engineers by way of identifying where they publish and what they cite.

3. It is a scientific discipline which performs reproducible measurements of scientific activity and reveals its objective quantitative regularities" (Haiturn).

Search Engine (SE)

1. It is a tool for finding, classifying and storing information on various websites on the internet. It can help in locating information of relevance on particular subject by using various search engines. (J. Rowley).

2. Encyclopaedia Britannica defines it as a "Computer Programme to find answers to queries in a collection of information, which might be a library catalogue or a database but is most commonly the World Wide Web. A web search engine produces a list of 'pages' computer files listed on the web that contain the terms in a query. Most search engines allow the user to join terms with 'and' 'or' and 'not' refine queries. They may also search specifically for images, videos or news articles or for names of websites". Examples: Google, MSN, Teoma,

Wise Net, AltaVista, Go.com and Lycos.

3. "It is a programme that allows users to locate specified information from a database or mass data. Search engine sites are extremely popular on the WWW because they allow users to quickly sift through million documents on the internet. (Computer Dictionary).

Types : 1. Individual search engines, 2. Subject Directories, 3. Meta-search Engine, 4. Free Text Search Engines, 5. Index Search Engines.

Features : 1. SE should contain comprehensive information broad areas, 2. It should be indexed on field of full text, URL, title bearer and weighted word, 3. Should provide a hierarchical subject oriented guide, 4. It should have quick response time and higher precision and recall, 5. It should act as user friendly interface, 6. It regularly update the contents of the database.

Limitations : 1. Search Engines produce too many results, 2. The search result and up being out of data and the message URL not found, 3. Lack of consistency between different search engines.

Search Strategy

The study of theory, principles and practice of making and using search strategies and tactics.

Sears List of Subject Headings, 15th Edition, 1994

First published in 1923 and designed by Minnie Earl Sears (1873-1933) in deference to demands of small libraries, thus the book is a standard subject cataloguing tool. Its 2nd and 3rd Editions were published in 1926 and 1933 under the editorship of Sears. The 4th (1939) and 5th (1944) editions edited by I.S. Munro also included DDC numbers. The 6th (1950), 7th (1954) and 8th (1959) editions were edited by B. M. Frick. The 6th Edition incorporated Sears' name to assume its present title. In the 9th (1965) and 10th (1972) editions edited by B. M. Westby, the DDC numbers were dropped, to reappear again as of 11th (1977) edition. The 12th (1982) was last edition edited by Westby. The 13th (1986) edition edited by C. Rovira and C. Reyes was first to be an online form. The 13th edition also incorporated some changes to suit OPACs environment. The electronic-age reforms have continued through the 14th (1971) and the 15th Editions.

Secondary Document

Documents which gives information about or the description of a primary document or a set of such documents e.g. Bibliographic records, catalogues, bibliographies. These provide secondary information that is information on (Primary) information; it does not bring any new knowledge but just describes its sources.

Selective Dissemination of Information (SDI)

1. "Service with an organisation which concerns itself with the channelling new items of information from whatever sources, to those points within the organisation where the possibility of usefulness is connection with the current work or interests in high". (H. P. Luhn)

2. The provision of secondary information on a current basis and according to an established schedule to an individual or a group of users, on their specific fields of interest, expressed by internet profiles (UNISIST Document).

Components of SDI: 1. Construction of document file or database, 2. Construction of user profile, 3. Matching strategies and techniques, 4. Notification and 5. Feed-back or user's interaction.

Semantic Web

This was envisioned by Tim Berners-Lee, the inventor of WWW with an idea to design a web such that not only documents are linked together but meaning of information in the Web documents can also be recognized. He defined Semantic Web as "Web of data that can be processed directly or indirectly by machines. It is about reading, processing, transforming and assembling the data repositories and documents available on the internet into useful information".

Service Quality

It can be explained as the difference between user's expectations and perceptions of service performance and the reality of service. Service quality means being able to view services from the customers' point of view and then meeting the customers' expectation for service.

Shodganga

The Shodganga project was initiated by INFLIBNET Centre, Ahmedabad. It is a digital institutional repository containing theses and dissertations from Indian Universities. In June 2009, the UGC has made a mandatory regulation for all Indian Universities to submit soft copies of Ph.D. theses and M.Phil dissertation to the UGC for hosting in the INFLIBNET. The 357 Universities and 14 centrally funded technical institutes in India are taken membership through MOUs with the INFLIBNET Centre to participate in the Shodganga Project. The Shodhganga@INFLIBNET is set-up and implemented by using free and open software called D-space. According to the notification of the UGC, it is mandatory that every research scholar of all Indian Universities have to submit a softcopy / version of their theses and dissertations for availability as open access to Indian theses and dissertation to the academic communities of the world.

Shodhgangotri@INFLIBNET

UGC initiated Shodhgangotri, a repository of electronic version of synopses submitted to universities. It is created and maintained by INFLIBNET Centre to supplement and compliment Shodhganga, a repository of full-text theses and dissertations. This repository would reveal the trends and directions of research conducted in Indian Universities and it would also avoid duplication of research.

Benefits : 1. Topic / title shall be publically accepted as the first registered topic and others may not be able to claim the same title / topic, 2. Area of interest will be known to other peer researches, 3. After awarding Ph.D., metadata from Shodhgangotri can transferred with full-text to Shodhgana which is mandatory requirement as per the UGC guidelines on Ph.D., 2009.

Skill

1. "Ability or proficiency in a execution or performance, specific art, craft, trade or job also such as an art, craft, etc., in which one has a learned competence" (Webster's Dictionary).

Types of skills : 1. Management skills: Such as supervisory, Counselling, planning, decision making, financial, personnel, technology and management skills. 2. Technological skills: Such as computer operation, telecommunication medias, repackage of information, online search, access to digital collection, design of World Wide Web, etc., 3. Communication skills: Such as written, oral, interpersonal, human / public relation, an user orientation, etc. 4. Traditional skills: Such as acquisition, organisation, and dissemination of information. 5. Research and statistical skills: such as Analysis, synthesis, interpretation, consolidation, evaluation and assessment. 6. Other skills: Such as to understand social, economic political developments vis-à-vis professional work and development.

Smart Card

A smart card, similar in look and size of a credit card has an embedded micro-processor or memory chip or both, instead of magnetic strip commonly found on debit and credit cards.

This technology will have several applications in identification, authentication, access control, health care, finance, administration, etc.

Smart Library

It was advanced information and communication technology to provide information services. It will be equipped with new technologies to carter to the information needs of local citizens and the community at large. It will be smart in the way of service delivery and will evolve itself as a knowledge convergence centre capable of responding to various information demands.

Social Bookmarking

It is a method for Internet users to store, organise, search and manage bookmarks of web pages on the Internet with the help of metadata. In a social book marking system, users save links to web pages that they want to remember and / or share. These book markers are usually public and can be saved privately, shared only with specified people or groups, shared only inside certain networks or another combination of public and private domains.

Social Cataloguing

Firstly the ability to share the catalogue and inter act with others based upon shared item and secondly the enrichment or improvement of cataloguing description through either explicit cooperation in the production of cataloguing metadata or through analysis of important information architecture associated with the resources under cataloguing activity. Steele described such activity as a social phenomenon and its use in cataloguing activity, metadata description, discussing, folksonomies, social book marking, tagging and use of controlled vocabulary such as LC Subject Heading (LCSH) or Medical Subject Heading (MeSH) for information retrieval.

Social Citation (SC)

It refers to storing, sorting, classifying, sharing and searching through a collection of internet based book marked links of citable sources such as e-journals, news articles, academic studies and interviews. Its functions are similar and directly inspired by social book marking services but are intended to be used for the collection of academic and citable resources.

Social Customer Relation Management (SCRM)

It is "a philosophy and business strategy supported by a technology platform, business rules, processes and social characteristics, designed to engaged the customer in collaborative conversation in order to provide mutually beneficial value in a trusted transparent business environment. It is the firm's response to customer's ownership of the conversation". (P. Greenberg).

Social Marketing

It is the use of commercial marketing techniques to promote the adoption of a behavior that will improve the well-being of the target audience or of society as a whole. The very characteristic that distinguishes social marketing from commercial marketing is its purpose, that, the benefits accrue to the individual or society rather than marketer's organization that is pushing the information.

Social Media

1. It is defined as a group of internet-based applications that build on web 2.0. It facilitates generating and sharing of user-generated content. It uses modern ICT Systems to provide avenues through which people can share and manage content generated by themselves.
2. According to Mayfield "It is a group of new kinds of online media which shares the characteristics such as (a) Participation, (b) Openness, (c) Conversation, (d)

Community and Connectedness". He further identified basic kinds of social media as: 1. Social Networks, 2. Blogs, 3. Wikis, 4. Podcasts, 5. Forms, 6. Content Communities, and 7. Micro blogging.

3. "A group of internet based applications that build on the ideological and technological foundations of Web 2.0, and that allowed the creation and exchange of user generated content". (Kaplan and Haenlein).

Advantages : 1. Captures potential users of the library, 2. Helps students to use library, 3. Helps students in locating library resources, 4. Facilitates knowledge sharing among the users.

Disadvantages : 1. Too many social media tools, 2. Inadequate library staff and lack of training opportunities, 3. Lack of time to use social media., 4. Less interest among library staff in learning and utilizing social media.

Social Media Technology (SMT)

"It refers to web-based and mobile applications that allows individuals and organizations to create, engage and share new user generated or existing content in digital environment through multi-way communications" (Davis, C H. et al).

Social Media Tools

These tools permit users to share information, communicate among the professionals, build relationships, share pictures, video, etc. Facebook, LinkedIn, Mebo, My space, Whats App, Twitter, etc. are most useful tools for information communication.

Social Networking Site (SNS)

1. It is an interactive communication platform where people can connect with one another and share their thought, experiences, pictures, audio, video, chatting via

text messages, audio call, video call and getting information from others.

2. A social networking site is an online platform that allows users to create a public profile and interact with other users on the website. Social networking cites usually have a new user input, a list of people with whom they share a connection and then allow the people on the list to confirm or deny the connection. After connections are established, the new user can search the networks of connections to make more connections" (Technopedia.com).

Uses : 1. It can be syndicated, share reusing or mixed, 2. It facilitates syndication, 3. It lets people learn easily from and capitalize on the behavior of knowledge of others.

Social Networks – Usefulness

1. "Socialization by LIS professionals and keeping updated with the developments in the profession, 2. Quick spread of information, 3. Communication from librarians to patrons and from patrons to librarians, 4. Marketing of products and services the libraries offer, 5. Collaborative sharing of information, 6. Access to the latest information on various issues, 7. Managing R &D operations, 8. Facilitating decision making, 9. Imparting reference service, 10. Promotion of library events and 11. Cross-national study and mobility". (H. K. Kaul)

Social Software

Tom Coates defines social software as "software which supports, extends or derives added value from human social behavior message boards, music taste-sharing photo-sharing internet messaging, mailing lists, social networking".

Social Tagging

In Web 2.0 technology, social tagging is a new phenomenon in the organization, management and discovery of digital resources. In tagging system any one can participate in the process and assign keywords they prefer. These social tags assigned by majority of participants for the resources are treated as valuable vocabulary to organize and share resources within the community. The concept of social tagging is adapted by any information communities and presently vast amount of online information is operated by social tags as information discovering tool. (A. Mathes)

Soft Skills

1. "Soft skills are combination of people skills, social skills, communication skills, character or personality traits, attitudes, career attribute, social intelligence and emotional intelligence quotients among other that enable people to navigate their environment, work well with others, perform well and achieve their goals with complementing hard skills". (Wikipedia).

2. Desirable qualities for certain forms of employment that do not depend on acquired knowledge. They include commonsense, the ability to deal with people and apositive flexible attitude". (Collins English Dictionary)\. *See* Hard skills.

Software

It is a general term used to describe the types of programs or lists of instructions which are needed to enable the computer system to carry out the necessary processing. It may be defined as a set of programs for a computer. These programs instruct the computer how to process the input data and generate different outputs. The programs are the set of instructions that a computer executes to accomplish an assigned / specific task. They direct the computer through a series of activities.

Software as a Service (SaaS)

It is one of the types of service in cloud computing. In this applications software is delivered as service to end user who can access the program online using a web browser or any other suitable client. Here service provider licenses an application to customers either as a service on demand or through a subscription, in a 'pay-as-you-go' model or at no charge.

Space [S]

The Fundamental Category (FC) 'Space' denotes concepts, isolate ideas such as geographical location or place where the entity resides or where some event or action takes place in relation to an entity or entity set. For example: *Academic Libraries in India*. In the (MC) Library Science Academic Libraries [P] and India is space facet.

Space GL

An Indian Portal for space science grey literature is a proto-type conceptual model for the design of a Web Portal which provides access to space science grey literature. It acts as a central hub for holding records of space science grey literature from all geographical regions of India.

Features: 1. Can be accessed from internet and intranet, 2. Supports online registration of remote and local user, 3. Grey literature can be archived by the submitters from anywhere and anytime against pass word authentication, 4. All types of grey literature can be achieved at one place in Space GL, 5. Supports interactive integration of grey literature from multiple sources, 6. Allows user to locate grey literature through a single user interface, 7. Provide services to support the submission, description, searching, browsing, access, preservation and visualization of these documents.

Spatial Information System (SIS)

"It is a computer-based information system that capture, integrates, stores, processes data, e.g., edits, analyzes, organizes and presents data related or linked to location(s). Describes and displays geographic / spatial information in different forms and format and SIS applications provide tools to create interactive queries (i.e. user created searches) analyze spatial information, edit data, maps and presents the results of these operations". (A. Neelameghan).

Special Auxiliaries

These denote locally recurrent ideas / concepts and are applicable either in a limited range or restricted range of schedules. These are listed at various places under each main class and its divisions in the schedules. These are applicable only where indicated and the same notation may be used elsewhere with a different meaning. These are to be added suffixes to other numbers. These cannot be used independently.

Special Librarianship

"The branch of librarianship administering and evaluating books and non-book materials in specific limited fields of knowledge and disseminating the information contained therein to meet the needs of the particular institution or clientele". (The Librarian's Glossary and Reference Book).

Special Library

"A Library which is maintained by an individual, Corporation, Association, Government Agency or any other Group for the collection, organization and dissemination of information and primarily devoted to a special subject and offering specialized clientele" (Harrods's Glossary).

Spiral of Scientific Method

According to Dr. S. R. Raganathan, Scientific Method works like never ending circle and conceptualized a 'Spiral of Scientific Method' in order to explain the steps and phases involved in scientific methodology. It means scientific research never ends and it is a continuous process. It identifies a problem, formulates hypothesis, verifies them, makes generalization and thus solves the problem.

Standard

It is a technical specification or other document containing a set of conditions to be fulfilled. This may be issued by companies, associations or groups, government departments, national standards organizations or regional or international standards bodies. (e.g. BIS, India, ISO, Geneva).

Standardization

It is the setting up by authority or common consent of a quality, quantity, pattern, method or unit of measurement for adoption as a common minimum or as an example for imitation. (P. Atherton).

Importance: 1. To bring uniformity and order, 2. A guide for establishment of new libraries and for the improvement of existing libraries, 3. A guide to the level of financial, material and human support, 4. Essential for planning and evaluation of library services, 5. To upgrade substandard libraries with yardsticks by which to measure their deficiencies.

Stock Verification

It is denoted by other terms as 'stock taking', 'stock checking', 'stock inspection' and 'inventory taking'. It refers to the process of checking as to what is in stock in relation to what there was. In library situation it is periodic verification of books and other reading materials of the library.

Advantages: 1. Periodic stock verification and writing off of resultant loss helps to reduce unnecessary escalation in the value of assets, 2. Helps in replacing relevant, useful and on demand documents with new copies / editions wherever loss, damage or mutilation occurred, 3. It helps in reviewing the precautionary measures taken in preventing loss of library materials, 4. Libraries can find deficiencies in the precautionary measure already taken.

Social Network

1. "A dedicated Website or other application which enables users to communicate with each other by posting information, comments, messages, images, etc." (Dictionary.com).

2. "A Social Network is a social structure made up of individuals (or organizations) called nodes which are tied (connected) by one or more specific types of interdependency such as friendship, kinship, common interest, financial exchange, dislike, sexual relationships or relationships of beliefs, knowledge or prestige. With the growing needs of networking among internet users and enterprises to create a common ground to communicate and share information with each other, a lot of open source social networking platforms are building which provide great opportunity for enterprise social networking" (Daniel Torres).

Social Networking (SN)

1. It is a "group of interrelated technological applications that is rooted on ideological and technological foundation of Web 2.0" (Kaplan and Haenlein). "Knowledge networking that indicates a number of connections, resources and associations that enable them to interact and share knowledge for the purpose of creating value among themselves" (Seufert et al). It will promote adequate information access, sharing and dissemination which are core functions of libraries. It allows users to join, create user pages (necessary information with a profile picture) invite and accept friendship requests from other uses of the system as a social friend. It also allows users to share ideas, thoughts, user generated contents (texts file attachments, photos, videos, music, etc) with others.

2. "An online space that allows people to connect, share,

communicate, establish or maintain connection with others". (Finin, Ding and Joshi)

Strategic Planning (SP)

It is a management tool like any other management tools. It is ued for one purpose only, to help an organization to do a better job to focus its energy, to ensure that members of the organization are working towards the same goals, to assess and adjust the organization's direction in response to a changing environment. In essence SP is a disciplined effort to produce fundamental decisions and actions that shape and guide what an organization is, what it does and why it does it, with a focus on future.

Subject Gateways

1. Lorcan Dempsey defined subject Gateways as "internet services which support systematic resource discovery. They provide links to resources (documents, objects, sites or services) predominantly accessible via the internet. The service is based on resource description. Browsing access to the resource via a subject structure is an important feature".

2. According to I Mesh Toolkit Project "A Subject gateway is a website that provides searchable and browsable access to online resources focused around a specific subject. Subject gateway resource description are usually created manually rather than being generated by hand, they are usually superior to those available from a conventional web search engine".

3. "Subject Gateways are Internet services which support systematic resource discovery. They provide links to resources (documents, objects, sites or services), predominantly accessible via the Internet. The service is based on resource description. Browsing access to the resources viz. subject structure is an important feature".

Different Names : 1. Information Gateways, 2. Subject based information Gateways, 3. Subject based Gateways, 4. Subject trees, 5. Virtual Libraries and 6. Clearing houses.

Characteristics : 1. An online service that provides links to internet. 2. Manual creation / invention, often by information and/ or subject specialists, 3. Selection of resources according to published quality and scope criteria, 4. Intellectually produced content descriptions ranging in length from short annotation to review, 5. Search and browse access and 6. Collection management policy supported by maintenance and updating procedures.

Subscription-based Article Delivery Model

No libraries can buy all journals due to affordability constraints even from specialty publishers in their subject area. Users approach to published content is rarely by journal but more by their topics of interest and study needs. Every publisher knows that subscription model limits the access to users for articles from his other non-subscribed journals by the library, but has rarely ventured into develop article delivery model as a parallel and equally remunerative business model comparable to subscription model. Of late as a means of making the article delivery model affordable, a few publishers have started bundling article delivery through subscription model.

Subscription Model

This model is perceived to be similar to libraries subscribing to journals with many variants in the right of access. It is most confusing model due to too many varied practices by publishers in setting the terms of licensing. It is a hybrid model of both perpetual access rights and limited access rights.

Suchika (Ver 1.0)

It is an integrated software package for library

automation designed and developed during 1996 by DESIDOC, Delhi for its Defense Science Library and other libraries / technical information centers (TICs) of DRDO scattered all over India. The purpose of developing this software is to automate all the DRDO libraries / ITCs, to create and maintain a DRDO libraries holdings' database and help the libraries to follow uniform standard practices. The package has been developed in C++ language in MS-DOS and UNIX versions keeping in view the requirements of big and small libraries of DRDO. The package is menu driven and user-friendly. The package conforms to international standards like CCF, ISO-27098, AACR-2 and allows data conversion from CDS/ISIS etc.

Super Computers

There are very large and sophisticated computers with extremely large data storage capacities, equipped with multiple set of very large processors. These are used when high speed, real-time, accurate computing is needed for example weather forecasts, scientific computation, missile navigation, etc., PARAM computers are produced in India.

Swayam

It is a programme initiated by Government of India and designed to achieve the three cardinal principles of educational policy: viz., access, equity and quality. The objective of this effort is to take the best teaching learning resources to all, including the most disadvantages. It seeks to bridge the digital divide for students who have hither to remain untouched by the digital revolution and have not been able to join the main stream of the knowledge economy.

Syndication

It means "the distribution of a news article through a syndicate in this case an RSS [Really Simple Syndicate] feed for publication in a number of newspapers or periodicals simultaneously. Used in the context of RSS syndication is all about distributing content for reuse or redistribution on other Websites" (Web definition).

System

1. A system can be defined as a network of interrelated procedures that are joined together to perform an activity or to accomplish a specific objective". It can also be defined as "an assemblage of objects united by some form of regular interaction or inter-dependence.
2. It is a set of elements — people, things, concepts, etc. which are related to achieve a common goal. It is an organized or complex whole, an assemblage or combination of things, or parts forming a complex or unitary whole. E.g. Mountain systems, River Systems, Solar System, etc.

Systems Analysis

1. It is both an approach to problems and a body of techniques to aid in their solution. As an approach, it follows the long history of scientific management theory; as a body of techniques, it draws mathematics, operations, research and the use of the computer (P. Atherton).
2. "A formal procedure for examining a complex process or organization, reducing it to its component parts and relating these parts to each other and to the unit as a whole in accordance with an agreed upon performance criterion".

Systems Analyst

A person who can start with a complex problem, break it down logically and identify the reasonable solutions. The analyst can study an ailing stem and come up with superior alternatives. He views a systems situation in terms of its scope, objectives and the organization frame work. In a library situation the Systems Analyst Performs of following functions:

1. Assisting management in the review and evaluation of operations and services, 2. Designing and implementing in cooperation with supervisory staff new or improved operating systems, 3. Conducting training programs for staff management, 4. Keeping abreast of new developments in data processing.

Systems – Approach

"Work pertaining to a man-made system predominantly involves (1) Systems-Design or System-Synthesis; and (2) Systems-Evaluation. Both these operations are based on a basic operation known as Systems-Analysis. All these activities call for strategy known as "Systems – Approach". "Systems-Approach" consists of applying a synthetic mode of thought as well as an analytic mode of thought for carrying out all the operations comprehended by the term "Management Activities" (G. Bhattacharya).

T

TROO DON

This software was developed and launched in the market by Comtek Service Pvt. Ltd., in the year 2000. This was multi-user in windows NT/Novell Netware Server. It was based on CCF for import / export data. The standard package has in all 7 modules: 1. Acquisition, 2. Circulation, 3. OPAC, 4. Serial Control, 5. Maintenance, 6. Backup and 7. Set up. The software was sold at Rs.1,10,000 to Rs.1,50,000. The company under takes data entry job of books at a minimum cost of Rs.2.35 per record. The software also provides customization as per local needs.

Tag Clouding

A tag cloud is text based visual representation of set of

tags which usually depicts tag importance by font size and / or font colour. A tag cloud provides users with comprehensible over view on the content of large tagged repositories. Each of the individual tag links to relevant subsets of repository content and tagclouds act as an instrument for topical browsing of the content. Tag Clouds occupy a peculiar niche in the domain of visualization. Recent trends in social and collaborative software, social cataloguing and web based library and information management environment have greatly increased popularity of tag representation form.

Technical Writing

"Presentation of the essential features of scientific and technical subjects and issues in a way that will make them more understandable and easier to absorb by a wider audience" (Saracevic and Wood).

Characteristics : 1. Deals with a subject or topic, 2. Addresses specific target group, 3. Presents the contents in a language that is oriented towards a target group, 4. Presents the write-up in a form supported by well-designed illustrations and photographs wherever necessary, to draw attention of the targeted group and 5. Gates printed attractively" (Prof. S. Seetharama).

Principles of T.W.: 1. Accuracy, 2. Logical Presentation, 3. Simplicity, 4. Word Choice, 5. Style & Grammar, 6. Analogy, and 7. Sensitivity (Saracevic and Wood).

Technological Gate Keepers

In industries, companies and corporations some senior individuals hold key or star positions in the communication network because of the frequency with which others consult them for technical advice or consultation. These people have greater exposure to the published or unpublished literature of the outside world than their colleagues as these seniors attend frequently conferences, discussions, seminars, etc. Such people are called 'technological gate keepers" as these senior are consulted by their colleagues for information.

Technological Security

It refers to the security of library software, hardware, network security, server security data security, work stations security and electronic security systems as fire alarms, burglary protection and barcode, etc.

Techno Stress

1. "A modern disease of adaptation caused by an inability to cope with the new computer technologies in a healthy manner. It manifests itself in two distinct and related ways in the struggle to accept computer technology" (C. Brod).

2. "Any negative effect on human attitudes, thoughts, behavior and psychology that directly, indirectly results from technology (M. M. Weliand L. D. Rosen).

3. "A condition resulting from having to adapt to the introduction and operation of new technology, particularly when equipment, support or the technology itself is inadequate" (D. M. Nina).

Tele kiosk

A typically Tele Kiosk consists of personal computer, printer / scanner, modern telephone and an assistant. The objective of these Tele kiosks is to provide basic information services to the communities in villages and also provide means of communication with the rest of the world. These kiosks could play an important role in facilitating the socio-economic development in the villages.

Tertiary Document

Document resulting from the transformation of the available primary and secondary information in order to express or represent it in a way which better fits the users' needs. Physically the tertiary documents appear often as new ones and might be considered and processed in the same way as primary documents. The information these sources contain is called tertiary information.

Thesaurus

1. "A controlled vocabulary arranged in a known order a structured so that the various relationships among terms are displayed clearly and identified by standardized relationship indicators". (American National Standards Institute and National Information Standards Organization).
2. "A vocabulary controlled indexing language, formally organized so that apriorie relationship between concepts are male explicit" (J. Acitchison, Allan Gilchrist and D. Bawaden).
3. "A lexicon, more especially where words are grouped by ideas; a grouping or classification of synonyms or near synonyms; a set of equivalence classes of terminology" (Hrrod's Librarian's Glossary).
4. It is "a compilation of terms of a given information retrieval system's vocabulary arranged in some meaningful form and which provides information relating to each term that will enable the user of the information file to predict the relevance of responses to questions when this particular vocabulary control mechanism is used" (Allen Kent).
5. "Thesaurus is a controlled and dynamic vocabulary of semantically and generically related terms, which covers a specific domain of knowledge of vocabulary is dynamic if it allows continuous updating, particularly addition of terms representing new concepts" (UNESCO).

Purpose : 1. To provide a map of a given field of knowledge indicating how concepts or ideas about concepts are related to one another, 2. To provide a standard vocabulary for a given subject field, 3. To provide a system of references between terms which will ensure that only one term from a set of synonyms is selected, 4. By providing 'see', 'see under' and 'see also' cross references the terms are properly linked together so as to avoid duplicacy of term in search process, 5. To locate new concepts in a scheme of relationships with existing concepts, 6. To provide classified hierarchies so that a search can be broadened or narrowed systematically.

Merits : 1. Retrieval procedures can be extended to collaborations in many different areas, 2. It becomes possible to investigate differences in vocabulary between different subject areas, 3. It removes any possible differences in retrieval effectiveness between subject areas. 4. It becomes possible to investigate that retrieval effectiveness of a variety thesauri for a given collection.

Thoughtful Blog

It presents an individual or small group's thoughts on current subject that are less contingent and more philosophical.

Time [T]

The Fundamental Category (FC) Time represents isolate ideas or concepts such as: Millennium, Century, Decade, Year, Day, Night, Winter, Summer, Hour, Second and Soon. For example: India's Foreign Policy in 2010. In the (MC) Political Science, Foreign Policy is [E] and 2010 is Time Facet.

Toll-Free Number

These numbers begin with one of the following three digit codes: 800, 888, 877, 866 or 855. Toll-free numbers allow callers to reach businesses and / or individuals without being charged for the call. The charge for using a toll-free number is paid by the called party instead of the calling party. *Need for toll free numbers in libraries. 1. By the use of toll-free numbers users can resolve their query on cell phone, 2. By the use this facility users have portability of a library, 3. It provides any time, any place library service, 4. It is free of cost, 5. It saves time of the user.*

Topical Blog

It is often focused on a specific niche often a technical one. An example is a 'Google Blog' that posts only Google news. Many Web logs now allow different categories which mean a general blog can be modified to become a topical blog as per the needs of the users.

Total Quality Management (TQM)

1. It is defined as "managing the entire Organization so that it excels in all dimensions of products and services which are important to the customers" (R. B.Chese and N. J. Aquilino).

    Essential Components : 1. Customer focus, 2. Employees involvement and 3. Continuous improvement.

2. A system of continuous improvement employing participative management and centered on the needs of users" (Bernard – 1993).

3. "TQM is the combination of socio-economic and technical process towards doing the right things (extremely), everything right (internally) first time and all the time, with economic viability considered at each stage of each process" (Zaira&Jurow, 1991).

    Elements : 1. Quality, 2. Quality Control and 3.Quality Assurance.

    Principles of TQM : To enhance the library services through 1. Library brochure, 2. Library Orientation, 3. Inter Library loan facilities, 4. Smooth acquisition procedure, 5. Use of technology, 6. Training of Library Staff, 7. Motivation, 8. User based information services, 8. User surveys, 9. Improve signage, 10. Change of timings, 11. Orientation to new staff, 12. Improvement of physical layout of the library, 13. Publicity of new services, 14. Target services to specific groups.(A. Pramanik)

Principal Objectives : 1. Continuous improvement of the organization which will be equal to greater than that of any competitor, 2. Continuous and relentless cost reduction, 3. Continuous and relentless quality improvement.

Benefits of TQM : 1. Work itself becomes more interesting through greater involvement of employees, 2. Increase in general productivity, 3. Lower absenteeism because of greater job interest and satisfaction to employees, 4. Less grievances among employees, 5. All-round team spirit.

Trade Literature

A book or Pamphlet issued by manufacturer or dealer illustrating and described his goods or products and sometimes including or accompanied by a price list. Forms of trade literature: single sheet, fold-out, folder, pamphlet, book and loose leaf binders.

Traditional knowledge (TK)

It is a term generally used for knowledge that is generated in informal ways. It has been generally passed from one generation to other generation. It may be in the written form or transmitted orally. It can be held by individuals, communities or society as a whole. (M.Koning). World Intellectual Property Organization (WIPO) defines traditional knowledge as "the knowledge, know-how, skills and practices that are developed, sustained and passed on from generation to generation within a community, often forming part of its cultural or spiritual identity".

Types of TK

1. Recorded knowledge: It is often referred to as codified and is available mainly in the form of ancient texts and manuscripts. These are mainly in those languages which were used at the time of their origin.

2. Oral Knowledge : It is referred to that knowledge which is not recorded or codified. It is transferred only orally from generation to generation within a community. It needs more attention to identify and preserve as it is the basis of livelihood for many indigenous communities.

Traditional Knowledge Digital Library (TKDL)

It is a knowledge repository on Indian traditional system of medicine which includes: Ayurveda, Siddha, Unani Siddha and Yoga. It is collaborative project of Council of Scientific and Industrial Research (CSIR), Ministry of Science and Technology and Department of AYUSH (Ayurveda, Yoga and Naturopathy, Unani, Siddha and Homeopathy), Ministry of Health and Family Welfare.

Traditional Knowledge Digital Library (KDL) Project

This project "digitizes the documents of various Indian traditional medicine systems which are available in the public domain. These documents are in the form of ancient literature and other existing literature and rarely understandable to common people. The TKDL targets Indian System of Medicine viz: Ayurveda, Unani, Siddha and Yoga available in the public domain. This is being documented by shifting and collecting the information about from traditional knowledge from the literature existing in local languages such as Sanskrit, Persian, Arabic, Urdu and Tamil in digitized format and is available in five international languages which are English, German, Spanish, French and Japanese. Information comprising about 2 lakh formulations have been transcribed for realizing the objective of TKDL Project" (M.A. Ansari).

Training

The systematic development of employee's knowledge, skills, and attitudes that are required for an organization to meet its goals (A. S. Antai).

Turnitin (Anti-Plagiarism Software)

It is the world's leading cloud based software for assessing student work. Anti-plagiarism software is for the students / researchers to check their papers against possible sources of plagiarism. Turnitin is mainly for building better teachers to improve writing / research. It can be customized and delivered according to the unique needs of each institution. Trainer modules are also available to help to build internal, site level training capacity.

Twitter

It allows users to write short messages of up to 140 characters called tweets that can be read by anyone with access to their pages. Users can utilize the platform to type in short messages or status update and also to keep staff and patrons updated on daily activities like frequently updated collections.

Typo 3

Typo3 is a free open source CMS written in PHP for enterprise purpose on the Web and in internets. It offers full flexibility and extended ability while featuring an accomplished set of readymade interfaces, functions and modules. It can run on Apache or IIS on top of Linux, Microsoft Windows, OS/2 of Mac OSX.

U

The UDC Consortium and the New Revision Policy

In January 1992 FID ceased to have overall responsibility of for the scheme and passed this to a consortium of publishers. This Consortium is collectively responsible for funding, developing and managing the classification. It consists of six members who represent the major publishers of the classification – the British, Dutch, Belgian, Spanish and

Japanese Publishers, together with the FID, the original owners of classification. The technical direction is managed by them, at present through their appointed Technical Director and the development of the classification, though their ultimate responsibility is undertaken by the editor in Chief and such experts as are needed to develop revise and evaluate revisions on a contractual basis.

UGC-INFONET

The UGC-INFONET had been overlaid on ERNET infrastructure to provide assured quality of service and optimal utilization of bandwidth resources. The project is being funded by the UGC with 90% capital investment and 100% recurring cost during X Plan period. A joint Technical and Tariff Committee (JTTC) consisting of eminent experts in the country has been setup to guide and monitor the entire project. INFLIBNET Centre, an autonomous IUC of the UGC, is the nodal agency for coordination of UGC-INFONET and facilitate linkages between ERNET and the Universities. UGC-INFONET shall be stepping stone in the process promoting the quality of higher education in several ways.

Functions : 1. Cataloguing service, collection sharing, electronic content licensing, electronic content loading / presentation, Inter library loan / document delivery, ,preservation, storage facilities, training, union lists / shared online catalogues, Networking all academic institutions in the country.

UGC Infonet Digital Library Consortia

It was formally launched by Dr. A. P. J. Abdul Kalam, President of India in December 2003, soon after providing the internet connectivity to the universities in 2003 under UGC-INFONET Programme. The consortia provides current as well as archival access to more than 7000 core and peer review journals and 10 bibliographical databases from 26 publishers and aggregators in different disciplines.

UIGC-Infonet: E-Journal Consortium

In order to provide current literature to academicians, UGC has initiated UGC-Infonet to provide electronic access, over the internet, to scholarly literature in all areas of learning to the universities in India, under its 4000 + full text scholarly electronic journals from 25 publishers across the globe can be accessed. The consortium provides current as well as archival access to core and peer-reviewed journals in different disciplines. The whole programme has been implemented in three phase manner.

Key features: 1. The programme launched with the aim to get qualitative changes in higher educational institutions in the country by providing access to electronic contents, using the state-of-the-art technology, 2. The whole programme, initially, was funded by the UGC for the first three years, 3. INFLIBNET is working as a nodal agency to monitor the execution of the programme., 4. Up to December 2005 more than 100 universities were accessing E-Journals subscribed under E-Journals Consortium, 5. INFLIBNET is conducting various local, regional and national training and awareness programmes to improve the e-information literacy.

UNICODE

It is developed by UNICODE Consortium. The consortium is a group of software organizations like IBM, Microsoft, Xerox, Oracle, etc. and they came out with 16 bit code called it UNICODE, as it promises to cover all the world's scripts. The promising feature of UNICODE is, it can represent 65,536 characters. The first version of UNICODE came in 1991. After that two more versions came in and present one is Version 3.0.

UNIMARC

IFLA working group on Content Designators recommended in 1973 a SUPER MARC which was based ISBD.

This was later called MARC International Format (MIF) from which the UNIMARC was developed. The final format was published in 1977. It is a communication format which necessitates writing and maintaining of only two conversion programmes – one from national format to the UNIMARC and the other from the UNIMARC to the national format. It was decided that each country can have its national format, but it should be the responsibility of the national bibliographic agency in a country to translate the records from the national format to the UNIMARC for purposes of interchange. ISBD was accepted as the basis of descript data elements within this format. The second edition of UNIMARC was published by IFLA International office for UBC handbook with the intention of guiding the users in its application.

UNISIST (World Scientific Information System)

UNISIST was established within UNESCO as an intergovernmental programme originally designed to stimulate and guide voluntary cooperative actions by UNESCO member states and also by non-Governmental Organizations to facilitate access to and international flow and exchange of scientific and technical information. The programme had its origins in the late 1960s.

Broad Principles: 1. Unimpeded exchange of published or publishable information and data among scientists of all countries, 2. Hospitality to the diversity of disciplines and fields of science and technology, 3. Promotion of the interchange of published or publishable information and data, 4. Cooperative development and maintenance of technical standards, 5. Promotion corporative agreements between and among countries, 6. Assistance to countries which seek access to contemporary and future information services in the Sciences.

UNIX

The Operating System UNIX was developed on and for minicomputers but implemented on micro, mini and main frame computers from multiple vendors. UNIX has contributed significantly to the world of operating system design and implemented in R & D environment. It has become one of the most popular operating systems in the commercial market place developed by experience programmes it has wandered beyond those bounds sincerely in 1980s. Designed to aid in software development process, UNIX has been pushed into the everyday routine of non-programming users.

Unicode Cross-Language Information Retrieval System (UCLIR)

It is a tool for exploring multilingual documents using a range of approaches such as using morphological analyzer, implementing bilingual dictionaries and standardized encoding of different languages.

Union Catalogue

A common list of holdings of two or more libraries or information centres. Such a list, which can cover books, periodicals or any kind of document, is usually prepared in order to facilitate the location of, and access to, the documents, the operation of inter-library loans and the realization of acquisitions (UNISIST Document).

Union Digital Centres (UDCs)

These are the phenomenal achievements of vision 2021 and digital Bangladesh. UDCs represent service access innovation which is leveraging the government's service process simplification works. In other words UDCs are assisting rural grass-root population to access different movement, non-government and other information services as a result of innovations in ICT based services in service delivery.

Universal Availability of Publications (UAP)

A programme launched by the International Federation of Library Associations and Institutions (IFLA) with the purpose of examining the obstacles which impede the availability of published documents within or among countries.

Universal Bibliographic Control (UBC)

A programme launched by IFLA for the promotion of a world-wide system for the control and exchange of bibliographic information. It is meant for preparing a bibliographic record of each item locally, immediately after its publication, using an international bibliographic standard format and making it readily available for the users throughout the world. The bibliographic control at National or International levels is achieved by way of bringing out bibliographic control tools such as bibliographies, indexing and abstracting journals, citation indexes, etc.

Universal Copyright Convention (UCC), 1952

It was sponsored and developed by UNESCO as an alternative to the Berne Convention for those countries which disagreed with many provisions in the Berne Convention. The developing countries and the USSR (now Russia) felt that the strong copyright protections granted by Berne Convention unduly benefited western developed countries, the US and most of Latin American Countries. The Berne Convention Countries also became signatories to the UCC, so that their copyrights would exist in non-Berne convention countries too. This convention has become redundant after World Trade Organization (WTO) came into existence as an UN specialized agency.

University Library

"A Library or system of libraries established, supported and administered by a University to meet the information needs of its students and faculty and support its instructional, research and service program" (ALA Glossary of Library and Information Science).

Use

The word is used in the context of verb and a noun. The verb implies consumption, put into service or seeking information.

User 2.0

Any person who believes in sharing, contributing, harnessing others knowledge and allows others to harness his/her knowledge, discussing things participating in library service design, etc. can be considered as user 2.0. That individual may not be a frequent internet user. A physical library user may also exhibit these features. Library Services should be hospitable enough to accommodate these users as well.

User Education

1. It has been defined as an instruction which equips library users with the skills to enable them to be independent and become sophisticated users of libraries and teir resources.
2. Fleming defined user education "as various programmes of instruction, education and exploration provided by libraries to users to enable them to make more effective, efficient and independent use of information sources and services to which these libraries provide access".

Components of User Education : 1. Librarians introducing new students, 2. Librarians familiarizing users who have little or no information seeking skills, 3. Libraries educating users on how to find materials manually or electronically using on-line public access catalogues and CD-ROMs.

Need and Importance : 1. To acquire the academic learning techniques, 2. To increase academic performance, 3. To help in quick decision making and problem solving, 4. To make the user self-reliant in making use of the library, 5. To keep the user community up to date, 6. To increase the visibility of information centres, 7. To bring awareness about the services of the library and information centres and 8. To surf useful websites.

User Interface

It means those aspects of the system that the user comes in contact with. It is those parts of the system the user actually sees and it follows that the user interface is responsible for making the functionality of the program accessible to the user and also the possibilities and limitations of the system. The degree to which this responsibility is fulfilled is called as the usability of the user interface.

Users

The whole community of those who might need at one time or another, information. It includes policy makers, decision makers, research and development workers, scientists, engineers, professors and students at all levels, workers in agriculture, industry, the services or in any other areas for which information can help to improve methods, products or results. (UNISIST document).

User research

It means not only gathering and documenting the information regarding the end users requirement but also involving the stakeholders in the domain of interest through various phases of the design process and also using information as a basis for the design and development of the system.

User Studies

It is to understand the users characteristic features, needs, preferences, practices, opinions, attitudes, behavior, etc. for evaluating library and information services that are offered. The aim is to help in designing, modifying, evaluating and improving the efficiency and effectiveness of LIS systems in order to meet their predetermined goals.

Objectives : 1. To identify the potential users and categorize them, 2. To identify the information requirements of user community, 3. To identify existing resources and services so that comprehensiveness of information can be achieved. 4. To evaluate various existing services and facilities in respect of their utility to users and achieve overall improvements in information systems from the feedback obtained from the users.

Users' Survey

It is a specialized type of investigation which is done to find out the reaction / opinion of the user community to a service or set of services offered by a library with a view to improve the library services. In the trinity of a library — books, staff and readers, the richness or weakness of the collection and services frequently used by him. User's opinion about the collection and services, therefore, are of paramount importance. User's opinions can be helpful to evaluating the strength or otherwise of collections and services. This is ascertained by conducting users' surveys.

Uses of Social Networking Services

These include: developing library resources, connecting staff with users, searching library catalogues and other online resources, providing user education, creating awareness of library resources, connecting with other librarians and library staff, getting feedback on library and its services, etc.

V

Value of Information

Some of the important values of information are:

1. Improved capability of a country to take advantage of existing knowledge, 2. Rationalization and systematization of a country's research and development efforts, 3. Wider knowledge base for the solution of problems, 4. New alternatives and approaches to the solution of technical problems, 5. Improved effectiveness and efficiency of technical activities in the production and service sectors, 6. Better decision making in all sectors and at all levels of responsibility. (P. Atherton).

Video Surveillance

Closed Circuit Television System (CCTV) is another way to monitor security and ensure safety. CCTV surveillance security can be adapted to libraries in identifying the visitors and employees. This video surveillance system records second by second movements of the visitors passing through the entrance / exit gate or via security bars when focused on such areas. Advances made in this CCTV technology reduced buying costs and available today for less costs.

Vidyamitra

It is an online learning portal. E-contents developed and supervised by NME-ICT (National mission on Education through Information and Communication Technology), MHRD, Govt. of India. It provides facility to access search / browse all the hosted content wherein a learner can easily access the desired material including audio / video learning material, textual material, multimedia enriched materials through a single interface. Various resources such as: *e-Text (44450), e-Tutorial / Videos (66174), are available and 46515 under*

Graduates, 20487 post-Graduates and 4715 content learners are accessing the resources.

VidyaNidhi Project

The Departmentof Library and Information Science (LIS), University of Mysore undertook an ambitious project called 'VidyaNidhi Project' which aims to create an online database of all doctoral theses and dissertations published by Indian Universities. The Project wassupported by NISSAT. The University has begun its work in July 2003 on the task of digitizing around 30,000 theses in English And other Indian languages published every year by 300 Indian Universities and other autonomous educational institutions. The project is funded by Ford Foundation and is assisted by Microsoft in harnessing industry standard tools such as Unicode for handling non-roman scripts and the Web language, Extended Marking Language (XML). In the first stage 200 theses of Mysore University, many in Kannada have been digitized and placed on the projects website *www.vidyanidhi.org.in* for free access and download. A bibliographic database of over 40,000 records has been created.

Vidwan database

One of the objectives of INFLIBNET Centre is to create subject experts database that would benefit the research and scientific communities, government agencies and R & D Organizations in the Country. In 2012, with the financial support from MHRD, Govt. of India, the Centre launched VIDWAN, a premier subject expert's database and national research network in India that contains information about expert's background, contact address, skills and accomplishments of the individuals. The database provides support to researchers, scientists, respective organizations and Government agencies for finding similar experts in same subject areas.

Virtua (Integrated Library System)

It is an integrated Library System and a stand based fully integrated, flexible software and also features like FRBR (functional requirements for bibliographic records), update notifications through SDI, user reviews and ratings and a smart device interface to the catalogue.

Virtual exhibitions

These are innovative ways to publicize the services of the library. It is a sort of networked exhibition portal for connecting users by providing online events like seminars and conferences. Virtual exhibitions use 3D graphics, audio and video to replicate the feeling of attending the physical events without time and place restrictions. The exhibition might be an extension of physical exhibition or a web exhibition itself.

Virtual Information Centre (VIC)

1. "A system by which users access information that resides solely in electronic format on computer networks without respect to physical location of the information" (S.I. Pacific).
2. "A concept of remote access to networked world wide library and information sources. The library that disseminates rselectiveinformation directly to consumers, usually through electronic interaction" (Gopen).

Spsecial Feagtures : 1. Information access and retrieval becomes more collaborative, 2. Information gathering should be free of space constgraints, 3. Regular training and retraining is necessary in the new information environment, 4. The merger of information on I.T. media, 5. I.T. resources replace print materials.

Services : 1. Union Catalogues, 2. Online Catalogues of library / information centres, 3. Information supply / delivery / dissemination services, 4. Inter-library loan services, 5. E-mail services, 6. Reference / Information marketing services, 7. Electronic bulletin board services and 8. SDI/CAS.

Virtual Institution (VI)

It is an institution which is supposed to deliver the programme using the Internet for any network. The availability of computer and ability to access the Internet is one of the most important reasons for the development of virtual institutions.

Virtual Learning Environment (VLE)

It is a software system designed to support teaching and learning in an educational setting, as distinct from Managed Learning Environment (MLE) where the focus is on management. VLE will normally work over the internet and provide a collection of tools such as those for assessment (particularly of types that can be marked automatically such as multiple choices), communication, uploading of content, return of student's peer assessment, administration of student groups, collecting and organizing student grades, questionnaires, tracking tools, etc.

Virtual Library (VL)

1. It is the most effective and efficient way to keep current and up-to-date journals and publications for the staff and students. It reduces distance and greatest strength is ease of accessibility to users thereby have remote access to library collections anywhere in the world instantaneously from a single room with few computer work stations. (Saalaam & Okorie).

2. It is a library with title or no physical collection of books, periodicals reading space or support staff, but one that disseminates selective information directly to distributed library usually electronically. It is a library without walls, spread across the globe from where one is able to retrieve the whole world of information

through a properly networked workstation. Here the user gets the impression as if he is moving through a large library does not physically exist, yet the user is able to retrieve the information needed by him.

Advantages : 1. Ease of accessibility, 2. Low cost, 3, As intensive or extensive as desired, 4. Easy to update and expand and 5. Minimal hassle due to loss or non-return of borrowed items.

Disadvantages : 1. Sometimes not as accessible or portable as libraries compared of paper copy items. 2. Potentially difficult to non-technical persons, 3. Lack of feel like real book, 4. Under the roof of Internet, many acquire unwanted information, 5. Wanted specific information may not easily available.

Virtual Reality

"It is display and control technology that can surround a person in an interactive computer generated or computer-mediated virtual environment. Using head-tracked, head-mounted displays, gesture trackers and 3-D sound, it creates an artificial place to be explored with virtual objects to be manipulated" (Quoted by Tapan Bhattacharya).

Virtual Reference Service (VRS)

It is an internet based reference service where a user can ask question on-line where the user and the librarian communicate in real-time. It was computers and communication technology to provide reference service to users anytime and anywhere.

It is defined as "The provision of real-time personal assistance to patrons via web-based interactive software".

Benefits: 1. "Reaches users in and out of libraries / social inclusion, 2. Invites users into library, 3. Provides better remote service for users-real information need, 4. Adds online learning component – can work users through finding information themselves, as in face to face service, 5. Supports real-time immediate assistance, immediate gratification, 6. Extended library hours, 7. Prepare student / user for better usage of physical repositories / archives by confirming material, sending out finding aids regulations in advance; and 8. Takes the library to the users. (A. D. Khobragade and Shalini R. Lihitkar).

Visible Watermarking

In this process the information is visible in the pictures or video. Typically the information is text or a logo which identifies the owner of the media. The image on the right has visible watermark. When a television broadcaster adds its logo to the corner of transmitted video, this is also visible watermark.

Vocabulary Control device

It could be described as a controlled dynamic vocabulary of semantically related terms offering comprehensive coverage of a domain of knowledge. It is used in the subject characterization of documents and queries in information storage and retrieval system based on coordinate concepts.

Types : 1. List of subject headings, 2. Classification scheme, 3. Thesauro facet and 4. Classaurus.

W

WAP (Wireless Application Protocol)

It is a protocol for accessing information and services from wireless devices. It is an open specification that offers standard method of access to Internet based content and services from wireless devices such as mobile phones and PDA's (Personal Digital Assistants). It is defined and coordinated by the WAP Forum. The group produces the implementing wireless network applications.

WINISIS

It is a windows version of CDS/ISIS (Computerized Information Service / Integrated Scientific Information System). It is widely used as an information storage and retrieval software all over the world. It was developed by UNESXCO to meet the automation requirements of libraries and information centres particularly in developing countries. WINISIS includes all features and capabilities of the MS-DOS Version of CDS / ISIS. It can run under all windows versions. The most important feature of WINISIS is its capability to handle an unlimited number of databases, each of which may consist of completely different data elements sets. It performs various operations of a library like bibliographic databases for an in-house collection like books, theses, manuscripts, etc, and automating acquisition procedure, circulation control, serial control, serial holdings, cataloguing, OPAC, etc.

Web

It is a synonymous term for World Wide Web (WWW) or the Internet or the online. The Web is a client or server system used to access all kinds of information by anyone on the net. The information can be in the form of regular text, hyper text, pictures, sounds, unsent news groups and other types of data.

Web 2.0

This was conceptualized and coined by Tim O'Reilly in 2004 to give an understanding of the design pattern and business models for the next generation web software. Web 2.0 highlights the value of user generated contents. According to Wikipedia 'the term encapsulates the idea of the proliferation of inter connectivity and interactivity of web delivered contents.

Foundations : The following are some of new tools and technologies which form the foundation of Web 2.0. 1. RSS

(Relay Simple Syndication) 2. Wikis, 3. Blogs, 4. Comments functionality, 5. Streaming media audio and video formats, 6. Reviews and user driving rating, 7. Personalized alerts, 8. Web-services, 9. Social networking software, 10. Open access, Open Source, Open Content, 11. Social bookmarking and 12. Instant messaging.

Principles of Web 2.0 According to Tim O'Reilly and John Battelle, the following are some of the key principles of Web 2.0 applications: 1. The Web as a platform, 2. Data as the driving force, 3. Network effects created by architecture of participation, 4. The end of software adoption cycle, 5. Ease of picking up by early adopters and 6. Light weight business model enabled by content and service syndication.

Characteristics : 1. Visibility, 2. Findability, 3. Searchability, 4. Accessibility and 5. Flexibility.

Features : 1. Personalization, 2. Simplicity, 3. Interactivity, 4. User Participation, 5. Social Interaction, and 6. Collective intelligence.

Web 2.0 Technology

"A space that allows any one to create and share information online, a space for collaboration, conversation and interaction, a space that is highly dynamic, flexible and adaptable" (K. A. Coombs).

Web 3.0

It is "a collection of technologies that consist of semantic web, linked data, natural language processing (NLP), artificial intelligence, mash-ups & APIS. Regardless of the specific Technology the core idea behind Web 3.0 is that when your information is organized you can extract much more meaningful and actionable insight from that of information".

Web-based E-Book Portals

The following are some important-book portals:

1. Elsevier Science Direct : It is a Web Portal to offer secure and authenticated access to e-journals, e-books and other electronic resources from Elsevier, a World leading Publisher and Information Provider.

2. Project Gutenberg : It is the first and largest single collection of free electronic books. Michael Hart, founder of the project Gutenberg invented e-books in 1971. Presently there are 17,000 e-books online.

3. Digital Library India : It is a national attempt to foster creativity and free access to human knowledge. The portal hosted by Indian Institute of Science, Carnegie Mellon University, ERNET, Ministry of Communications and IT and 21 participating Centres of the Government of India. There are about 50,000 of books accessible on Web.

Web-based Information Resources

These resources are also known as internet information resources. These resources may be categorized as Websites, portals, online courses, list serves, special internet groups, virtual conference, chat, e-journals, e-books, mailing list, multimedia collection, web links, map collection, online bookshop, sound, etc. The most popular information resources used by students are search engines and subject-related data bases.

Web based instruction (WBI)

"Using the World Wide Web (WWW) as the medium of conducting courses for students". Instructions and professors are putting up content in WWW at an increasing rate. The software developers are responding by creating software that facilitates the creation of web based instructions.

Web based library instructions

Library professionals should organize programs for their user community to make them well aware about different information resources and the services provided by the LICs.

The instructions can be put on the Website of the parent institution so that users can understand the rules and regulations they are supposed to follow and know the skills for making optimal use of library resources and services.

Web Browsers

These are software programs that allow accessing the graphical portion of the Internet, the WWW. The first browser, called NCSA Mosaic was developed at the National Centre for Super Computing Applications. The easy-to-use point-and-click interface helped popularize the Web. Web browsers are loaded with a number of features. Most browsers allow to: *View Web pages, Create Web pages, Add Multimedia components, Link from one document to the other, Download information, Access databases and Access and download freeware / shareware programmes.*

Web-Casting

It is a live media file distributed over the Internet using streaming media technology. Essentially, Web –casting is broadcasting over the Internet. More generally, it is referred to as transmission of linear audio or video content over the Internet. A Web-casting uses streaming media technology to take single content source and distribute it to many simultaneous listeners / viewers.

Web-based OPAC

It allows multidimensional searches through different access points depending upon customization, software, need or demand of an organization.

Features : 1. Offers libraries the opportunities to have access to various resources of their libraries on the Web, 2. Allows users to interact with documents stores in computers all over the World, 3. Makes easier to access catalogue data in the form of bibliographic records, 4. Has the ability to search OPACs of other libraries, 5. Powerful tool to link all the electronic resources of other libraries and 6. It becomes another search engines.

Web Crawler

It is "a Program or automated script which browses the World Wide Web in a methodical automated manner" (Kobayashmi and Takede). Other less frequently used names crawlers are ants, automatic indexes, bots and worms. Most of the search engines use Web Crawler as a means of providing up-to-date data.

Web hosting

It is one of the earliest adoptions of cloud computing as many organizations including libraries preferred to host their websites on third party service provides rather than hosting and maintaining their own servers. Google sites serves an example of a service for hosting websites outside the library's servers and allowing for multiple editors to access the site from varied location. Operated by companies known as web hosting providers or simply web hosts these services are managed out of data centres facilities and made available to personal and business customers in various regions throughout the world.

Types of Web hosting : 1. Free Web-hosting service, 2. Shared Web-hosting service, 3. Reseller Web hosting, 4. Virtual dedicated server, 5. Dedicated hosting service, 6. Manage hosting service, 7. Cloud hosting, 8. Grid hosting and 9. Home Server.

Webliography

It is an enumerative list of hypertext links and a gateway to the scientific sources of information on the Net, whether annotated or not. Webligraphies are in fact digital equivalents of bibliographies (Printed list of information sources). Bibliographies are secondary sources information among print media and webliographies are the same on the Net.

Importance: 1. Provide access to relevant information, 2. Users can quickly access Webligraphies and use these links to find information, 3. Can be useful for remote library users, 4. Provide access not only to textual information as in print but in multimedia that is more advantageous.

Web-log

1. "A Web-log, or blog is a web-application that is designated to be updated with periodic posts in a linear, time-based manner, similar to a dairy or personal journal, except that the contents are meant for public consumption" (D. Kline and D. Burstein).
2. "Blog / weblog: a page containing brief, chronologically arranged item of information. A blog can take the form of a diary, journal, what's new page or links to other web sites" (Peter Scott).
3. "A Weblog journal or newsletter that is frequently updated and intend for general public consumption.

Characteristics: 1. Easy to distribute the content, 2. Communicating within the building, 3. Interactive, 4. Open access feeling, 5. Promote Library and Information Centre's events, 5. Support dedicated users, 6. Engage user community and 7. Make announcement of the parent organization.

Advantages: 1. No need to know HTML, FIP, 2. Add/ Edit content any where, anytime, 3. Dynamic, quick and easy to develop, 4. Easy to publish, 5. No need to download software and 6. Open source and open access feeling.

Webology

It is an international peer-reviewed open access journal in English devoted to field of World Wide Web (WWW) and serves as a forum for discussion and experimentation. It serves as a forum for new research in information dissemination and communication process in general and in the content WWW in particular. Besides, Webology is by Scopus, ProQuest, LISA,

DOAJ etc. The Journal is listed in the online catalogues and directories of open access journals of several prestigious university libraries around the world. It is a publication of Regional Information Centre for Science and Technology, Iran.

Webometrics

1. The term was first coined by Almind and Ingwersen. The science of webometrics tries to measure the World Wide Web to get knowledge about the number and types of hyperlinks, structure of WWW and usage patterns. Bjorneborn and Ingwersen defined it as "the study of the quantitative aspects of the construction and use of information sources, structures and technologies on the web drawing on bibliometric and informatric approaches".

2. "The Study of Web-based content with primarily quantitative methods for social science research goals using techniques that are not specific to one field of study". (Thelwall Mike).

It is an advanced information parameter that emphases on quantitatively describe web characteristics. Web characteristics mean the pattern of use by website users, the number of website links, structure and other website reciprocal links.

Webopedia

It is a free online dictionary for words, phrases and abbreviations that are related to computer and Internet technology. Webopedia provides easy-to-understand definition in plain language avoiding the use of heavy jargon wherever possible so that the site is accessible to users with a wide range of computer knowledge. In addition to a definition of the term or phrases webopedia also provides links to sources of further information on the topic where applicable.

Webpage

The documents that are available in the computers connected to Internet are called Web documents or Webpages. Webpage is a single unit of a document. The length of it may be long or short depending upon the information it holds. The collection of webpages of a single library, organization or institution is called website and the very first page of such a website is called as Home Page. Every Website has its address and this address in computer terminology is known as Uniform Resource Location (URL).

Webpage for a library: Advantages: 1. Opportunity to interact with user community, 2. Collections and services offered by a library for user community can be put before them with minimum cost, 3. Less expensive and very effective media, 4. Takes less time to reach the user community, 5. Provides extraordinary combination of cost effectiveness, 6. Acts as a mirror for the library, 7. Current developments in the library can be communicated to the user community within a short period and 7. Users can download the information of the library on their computer very quickly and effectively.

Web Protocols

The three protocols that are core to WWW are the : 1. Hyper Text Markup Language (HTML) that specifies a simple makeup language for describing hypertext pages, 2. Hypertext Transfer Protocol (HTTP) which is used by Web browsers to communicate with Web clients and 3. Uniform Resource Locators (URLs) which are used to specify links between documents.

Web Searching

It is an interaction between an individual and a database, where the individual states his query in the form of search terms and logical combinations of search terms, to retrieve small sets of very specific information, from large computer stored database. It can also indicate the search services available from producers of databases or vendors or suppliers of these databases.

Web Technology

It is software, hardware and network architecture that use standards and technologies developed for the internet and the World Wide Web (WWW). WWW is major service on the internet. The WWW is made up of 'web servers' that store and disseminate 'web pages' which are rich documents that contain text, graphics, animations and videos to anyone with an internet connection. The heart of Web technology is the hyperlink which connects each document to each other whether locally or around the world by clicking link.

Types: 1. Internet, 2. Intranet, 3. Extranet, 4. Webpages, 5. Web services, 6. Portals / Gateways / Routers, 7. Search engines, 8. Email, 9. Internet Forums and 10. Peer to peer communication.

Weeding

1. "Weeding is the process of removing material from open access and reassessing its value" (International Encyclopedia of Information & Library Science).
2. "Removing the non-core collection, from the primary collection area" (S. S. Stole). It is a kind of process which helps to remove damaged, old and less-used library collection from the stacks.

Reasons: 1. To serve space, 2. To improve access and 3. To save money (Evans).

WhatsApp

This was developed in 2009 by Brian Acton and Jan Koum. It is a proprietary cross-platform, encrypted, instant messaging application for smart phones. It uses the internet to send text messages, videos, documents, user location, contacts and other users using mobile number. It runs over various operating systems such as: IOS, Android, Windows OS, Mac OS, Black Berry OS etc.

Advantages : 1. Free messenger application, 2. Widely used by people to send multimedia messages like photos, videos, audios along with simple text messages and voice calls as well as video calls, 3. Its application is being treated as teaching learning tool, 4. It is used in higher education for interaction among students, and for sharing learning material, 5. This application runs only through standard mobile devices with internet connections.

Wi-Fi

Wi-Fi is short for "Wireless Fidelity". It is a term that refers specifically to wireless local area networks utilizing the standards spelled out in the IEEE 802.11 specification. The term Wi-Fi has been promulgated by the Wi-Fi alliance, a non-profit group of manufacturers.

Wikipedia: The free encyclopedia

It has been observed that the present century is the pioneer for open access movement and is a large scale collaborative content development model. This model has been enabled by Internet based content development and management technology specifically by 'Wiki engine' system. One of the most important products of this technology is the online open access encyclopedia called *"Wikipedia: the free encyclopedia"*. Not only it provides the free online encyclopedia contents but also revolutionized the model of encyclopedic content development as anybody can contribute an article as well as edit or improve and refine its contents.

Wikis

It is a term used variously to either refer to a collaborative website where users can create, edit or delete content using a web browser or it may refer to software used to run a wiki website. Ward Cunningham first developed the Wiki Software and hosted the first Wiki Website called Wiki Wiki Web. The important features of wiki are: 1. *A wiki website allows its users to create, edit or delete content, 2. Provides meaningful page links between relevant pages.*

Windows NT Operating System

In 1988 Bill Gates commissioned the creation of a new operating system. The premise for the design of this new operating system was portability, security, compliance and compatibility, scalability, and extensibility. The system should need to run on different hardware platforms with minimal changes. It could be locked down through software, meeting NSA's C2 level criteria.

Wisdom

It implies the application of knowledge as contained in human judgment centered around certain criteria or values that are generally accepted by the culture or society. Wisdom can be thought of as knowledge applied.

Word Press

Word Press is an open source blog publishing application powered by PHP and MySQL which can also be used for basic content management. It has many features including a user friendly workflow, a rich plugin architecture and an advanced template system.

Word Processing

It was one of the first major applications of computers. Word processors are basically text processing packages used to create error-free alternative looking documents. With a word processor, the keyboard is used to enter a document into the computer. Typographical errors can be corrected by simply backspacing and retyping the entry correctly one can insert new phrases and delete superfluous material. A powerful set of editing commands will move words, sentences, or even paragraphs from one place to another. Additional programs, check spelling, improves grammar, provides intermediate access to thesaurus and send form letters.

Work Culture

It is an integrated system of learned behavior by the workers or employees in their work place within an organization. The organization has to depend upon its work culture to attain its goals and objectives. In case of a library which is a non-profitable social organization effective service of the organization to the clientele depends upon the work culture it maintains.

Work Motivation

"An environment which effects our direction and maintenance of behavior in pertinent work settings". (O. P. Verma). Motivation is the force to behave towards a goal or possible goals or set of values of the organization. It may be viewed as commitment related.

Work Place Learning

It is a process whereby employees acquire knowledge, skills and attitudes that enhance their individual performance and organizational tasks. It comes as a result of autonomous self-directed learning by employees to satisfy their organizational needs at the work place. (E. Hicks et.al and R. Holliday).

Work Study

"It is generic term for those techniques, particularly method of study and work measurement which are used in the examination of human work in all its contents and which lead systematically to the investigation of all factors which effect the efficiency and economy of the situation being reviewed in order to effect economy" (ILO).

The World Intellectual Property Organization (WIPO)

The convention to establish WIPO was signed at Stockholm on July 14, 1967. It has its headquarters in Geneva and it is a specialized body of UNO.

Objectives

1. To promote the protection of I.P. throughout the world through cooperation among member States,
2. To ensure administrative cooperation among the unions.

Functions

1. To promote the development of measures designed to facilitate the efficient protection of I.P.R. throughout the world,
2. To perform administrative tasks of Paris Union, the Special Union established in relation with the Union, and the Berne Union.
3. To encourage the conclusion of international agreements designed to promote and protection of I.P.
4. To offer its cooperation to States requesting legal-technical assistance in the field of I.P.
5. To assemble, disseminate information concerning the protection of I.P.
6. To maintain services facilitating the international protection of I.P.

World Wide Web (WWW)

WWW is defined as the portion of the Internet whose pages are inter-connected by hyperlinks.

Characteristics: 1. Material stored on a web server can be accessed from any place; 2. Material can be consulted with any type of computer and with any browser; 3. Material can be accessed anytime; 4. Can show moving images animations, etc.; 5. Easy to update contents; 6. Users can share single copy; 7. Occupies less storage space; and 8. May be shipped over networks.

Major resource types : 1. Organizations; 2. Numerical data sets; 3. Dictionary, Encyclopedia, Directory and other Reference sources; 4. Electronic journals; etc. 5. Legal documents; 6. Current affairs, 7. E-commerce; and 8. OPAC.

Y

You Tube

It is a video-sharing website where in one can make available the content including video clips, T.V. Clips, music videos and also seminar presentations, education related videos like how to search books, OPAC, e-resources, repositories, etc.

Features and activities : 1. It is a resource for library service and information which can disseminate the video lectures, 2. All types of libraries are using it for self-development of users, 3. A free to use promotional platform for various levels of higher education, 4. Online Video learning can change the scenario of learning process.

Z

Z39.50 (Standard Information Retrieval: Application Services Definition and Protocol Specification)

It is an American National Standard and an open communication protocol. It specifies a standard way of communication between two systems for searching databases and retrieving information. It is platform independent i.e. it allows communication between two computers having different hardware and software. It allows uniform access to a large number of diverse and heterogeneous information resources. It allows searching multiple databases using a single, standard interface. It allows broadcast searching which means user can perform the same search simultaneously against several databases.